Praise for *Love*

M000033872

"My friend Michelle Adams' new book, *Love and Care for the One and Only You,* will lead you through a spiritual workout that will help grow your faith, refresh your spirit, and allow you to live a happier and healthier life."

Victoria Osteen, Co-Pastor of Lakewood Church

"*In Love and Care for the One and Only You,* you will find a new confidence in yourself as a treasured daughter of our Heavenly Father. This book is a game-changer!"

Pat Smith, Minister, Author, Founder of Treasure You and

Co-Founder of Pat and Emmitt Smith Charities

One of the biggest obstacles that women have to achieving better fitness is discouragement. Michelle Medlock Adams' words aren't just salve for a wounded or tired heart, they are spiritual nutrients, well blended to stimulate your faith endorphins. Michelle's book gives you encouragement, rich with joy to consume daily and Biblical wisdom that will stretch and strengthen your spirit with God's grace and power.

Brad Bloom, Publisher, *Faith & Fitness Magazine*,

FaithAndFitness.net

"Every church needs this. I want to do a Bible study using this book. This is an all-inclusive guide to caring for 'the one and only you.' This book is a perfect and pure blend of self-help tips with scripture."

Cindi Brand, Gym Owner and Certified Personal Trainer
Cindi Brand, Priority Fitness

"*In Love and Care for the One and Only You,* I could relate to so many of the struggles and obstacles we are faced with in life. Michelle's book is encouraging and uplifting from a physical and spiritual perspective."

Brenda Anderson, Independent Beachbody Coach

"Once you've read the witty, relatable stories and practical wellness tips in Michelle's *Love and Care for the One and Only You,* you'll be encouraged to take healthy steps to live as God intended. As a fitness and wellness expert and creator of the Visibly Fit™ exercise program, I believe that once your mind and spirit are in the right place . . . your body will follow! Michelle simply leads you step by step."

Wendie Pett, www.wendiepett.com

Love & Care
For The One and Only
YOU

52
Inspirations

MICHELLE MEDLOCK ADAMS

WORTHY®
Inspired

Published by Worthy Inspired, an imprint of Worthy Publishing Group, a division of Worthy Media, Inc., One Franklin Park, 6100 Tower Circle, Suite 210, Franklin, TN 37067.

WORTHY is a registered trademark of Worthy Media, Inc.

HELPING PEOPLE EXPERIENCE THE HEART OF GOD

Library of Congress Control Number: 2015953088

Cover design: Jeff Jansen / Aesthetic Soup
Cover Illustration: Getty Images

Printed in the United States of America

16 17 18 19 20 21 RRD 11 10 9 8 7 6 5 4 3 2 1

FOR JEFFREY—MY WORKOUT
PARTNER, MY BEST FRIEND,
MY BIGGEST CHEERLEADER,
AND THE LOVE OF MY LIFE

CONTENTS

. . . .

STRENGTH TRAINING

STRETCHING

INTRODUCTION

· ·

I RECENTLY READ a quote on Instagram that said, "Strong is the new skinny."

I like that a lot because I may never be a size 2 (in fact, I think I skipped that size growing up . . .) but I am strong. I am proud that I am physically strong—able to hold an abdominal plank position for several minutes; able to squat and lunge with the best of them; able to hike L.A.'s Runyon Canyon with my twenty-year-old daughter and live to tell about it!

I am woman, hear me roar!

But I wasn't always that way. In fact, after having surgery earlier this year, I could hardly climb the stairs in my house, let alone hike up a mountain! It's definitely been a year of recovery, rebuilding, and getting back into shape.

Maybe you can relate.

This journey of wellness is not one where we ever reach our destination and set up camp. I wish it were that easy. No, it's a daily journey—a journey where we put one foot in front of the other and keep moving toward total health—spirit, mind, and body.

And it all starts with God.

Trust me; I've tried getting to that happy, healthy, and fit destination every other way. There's no magic pill. There's no fad diet. There are no shortcuts.

There is only God, and He is all you need to succeed in every area of your life—including your health and fitness.

I don't care how many times you've failed in the past. I don't care how many pounds you've lost and regained over the years. I don't care if you can't walk to the mailbox without becoming winded. Your journey to a healthier, happier version of yourself begins today.

You can do this because you're not doing it alone!

You are strong in the Lord! He has empowered you to fulfill your calling on this earth, and He has strengthened you to withstand anything that life throws at you. Psalm 18:32 says, "It is God who arms me with strength and makes my way perfect" (NKJV). And, one of my favorite verses, Philippians 4:13 says, "I can do all things through him who strengthens me" (ESV).

You should shout a great big "Amen!"

You may not feel strong physically or spiritually, but we don't go by feeling, we go by faith. We call things that be not as though they were, and we believe that God's Word is true and alive and personal! When it says in Isaiah 40:29, "He gives power to the weak and strength to the powerless" (NLT), you can insert your name into that scripture.

You can say out loud, "He gives power to me! He gives strength to me!"

Because He does!

Look, we will probably never have the perfect bodies. But we can all rejoice over this truth—we are perfectly loved by Almighty God!

When we realize how valuable we are—so valuable that God sent His only Son to die for us so that we could spend eternity with Him—we will desire to take care of ourselves, spiritually, mentally, and physically. We'll want to get healthy—not so we can fit into our skinny jeans—but rather so we can have enough energy to accomplish all that He has planned for us.

You see, it's really not about us; it's all about Him.

Once you realize that truth, this journey of wellness becomes a joyful one.

Won't you take it with me?

WARM-UP

· ·

CHAPTER 1

AVOID THE COMPARISON TRAP

. . . .

A peaceful heart leads to a healthy body;
jealousy is like cancer in the bones.

Proverbs 14:30 (NLT)

RECENTLY WHILE TRAVELING from Asheville, North Carolina, to Indianapolis, I was perusing a copy of a women's magazine to pass the flight time when I came across a picture of Jennifer Aniston.

She looks amazing, I thought.

Then I read her age—*she's exactly my age!*

No way! How can this be? She looks like she could be in her midtwenties! Look at those abs!

Not only that, she has perfect skin and gorgeous hair, and she seems like the "girl next door" whom you would actually want to be friends with . . . (Insert sigh of hopelessness and discontent here.)

It was at that very moment, I fell smack-dab into the Comparison Trap.

Nothing against Jen—I am actually a big fan—but here's the reality: She is paid to look gorgeous. My good friend said it best, "Look, if I had a personal trainer to motivate me and help me get into shape and a personal chef to prepare healthy yet yummy meals for me every day, I could look amazing, too!"

Here's another dose of reality. I once helped a former model write her memoir, and she told me that even famous models are airbrushed and enhanced for magazines and catalogs.

Think about that for a moment. If these 5'10", 108-pound models, who are quite underweight by all recommended standards, are being Photoshopped to improve their "imperfections," when we see the final product in the pages of our favorite fashion magazines, their images are truly perfect . . . as well as perfectly unattainable.

In other words, we're being set up to fail. We look at their "perfect 10" bodies, and then we study our own physiques and think, *Well, forget this! I can never look like that, so I think I'll just drown my sorrows in a pint of mint chocolate chip ice cream.*

Ever been there?

It doesn't have to be a celebrity comparison that causes us to stumble on our journey to a fabulous, fit, and healthy version of ourselves. It might be a best friend who just lost thirty pounds and meets you for coffee wearing hot, skinny jeans, causing you to feel like "frumpy friend."

Don't be jealous; instead, celebrate her transformation. Be

inspired, not envious. And don't waste any energy comparing your backside to hers—it's a futile activity that will only end with another pint of ice cream.

That's why this comparison trap is so damaging. It can totally derail us. One discouragement detour leads to another, and before you know it, you've given up. So, ladies, stop comparing yourself to your BC (before children) self; stop comparing yourself to celebrities; and stop comparing yourself to your friends.

You are an original! You are uniquely wonderful! You are valuable! And, though you may not be the exact weight you wish to be or have the backside you once had at twenty-two, that doesn't make you any less valuable.

It's okay to have weight-loss goals—realistic, non-Photoshopped goals—and push forward to achieve a healthy, fit body, but comparing yourself to others will only make that journey less enjoyable.

It's time we start loving ourselves again. It's time we see ourselves through the eyes of our Heavenly Father. It's time we celebrate every inch of ourselves—even if there are more inches there than we'd like. It's time we strive for progress, not perfection.

Praise God that you have another day to live this amazing life. Praise God that you have the gift of eternal life because He sent His Son. Praise God that even though you're not perfect, you are perfectly loved by Him!

It's a great day to be alive, so go out and live it—free from self-loathing and the fear of judgment—and determine you'll never fall victim to the Comparison Trap again.

POWER PRAYER: *Father, help me to see myself through Your eyes. And help me to stop comparing myself to others and simply be the best version of myself. I love You, Father, and I'm thankful that You love me just the way I am. Help me to strive for progress, not perfection, and to enjoy the journey on the way to a happier, healthier me. In the Mighty Name of Your Son, Jesus, Amen.*

WORK YOUR WORDS: I will not get caught in the Comparison Trap. Instead, I will strive for progress, not perfection, and I will enjoy the journey on the way to a happier, healthier me.

HEALTHY HINT: Celebrate the little victories! In order to do that, you'll have to compare where you are today to where you've been and where you're going. But that kind of comparison game is a good one because you're celebrating progress. For example, if you have been walking thirty minutes every night for the past month and you can now zip up a pair of pants that you couldn't fasten before, celebrate that progress. Whoo-hoo! You might even want to start a Progress, Not Perfection Celebratory Journal to track your positive changes.

CHAPTER 2

GIMMICKS AND FADS AND LIES, OH MY!

. . . .

"I the LORD do not change."

Malachi 3:6 (NIV)

YOU KNOW WHAT SENDS women screaming from dressing rooms across America?

Bathing suit season.

Scary.

The thought of wearing a bathing suit in public makes normally sane women do really ridiculous things in order to lose a few pounds before bathing suit season.

I admit it—I am, occasionally, one of those women.

So, when I recently read on a magazine cover, "Eat a can of pineapple before you go to bed and speed up your metabolism!" I immediately ran to the store, purchased ten cans of pineapple, and began downing a can before bed each night. Of course, I didn't lose any weight and all of that acidic pineapple left my mouth with small blisters.

Later, I read in another magazine that drinking a spoonful

of apple cider vinegar before every meal would promote better health and weight loss. (The verdict is still out on that one . . . I'll let you know.)

And just the other day I saw a news report touting the amazing weight-loss benefits of Wu-Long tea. The article said it was safe and all-natural, so, as you might have guessed, I ordered some of that too.

It seems that every single day a "new and improved" product debuts and claims to be a great aid in promoting weight loss. Or a new study reveals that what we once thought was a good, safe, effective vitamin to aid in carb blocking is actually harmful to one's health.

It's hard to know what to believe!

Obviously, new information is discovered. New studies emerge. New products are invented. Sometimes, it seems almost impossible to keep up with current diet and health trends and differentiate between truth and myth. (I know because I write a lot of articles in the health and fitness market, and it's ever-changing!)

In a world of empty promises, crazy gimmicks, and bogus studies, aren't you glad that God's Word is true and that He never changes? I am so thankful that God is the same yesterday, today, and forever. I am so grateful that I won't wake up tomorrow and discover that grace is no longer available to me or that prayer works only on Tuesdays.

Yes, things are constantly changing in many areas of my

life (especially my body since I hit my midforties) but not in one—my relationship with God. He is my stability, my rock, my love, and my firm foundation. His love is never-ending. His favor is limitless. And His mercies are new and available to me every morning.

And guess what? They're available to you, too!

So if you're feeling a little frazzled, overwhelmed, or confused by all the craziness of the world or simply a little mortified that you actually wasted money on the "lose weight while you sleep" formula, spend some quality time with your Father today. You'll come away completely refreshed, assured of who you are in Him, and ready to face the day.

Now, I've got to run . . . the FedEx guy is here with my order of Wu-Long tea . . . for research purposes, of course. ;)

POWER PRAYER: *Father, thank You for being the same yesterday, today, and forever. I am so thankful that I can count on You—no matter what. Help me to trust You more, Lord, in every area of my life, and help me to develop better discernment. I love You. In the Mighty Name of Your Son, Jesus, Amen.*

WORK YOUR WORDS: I have great discernment, and I make healthy choices.

HEALTHY HINT: Instead of jumping on the "diet fad wagon," try eating a balanced diet of protein, carbohydrates, fats, and fiber.

CHAPTER 3

SET A GOOD EXAMPLE

. . . .

Train up a child in the way he should go;
even when he is old he will not depart from it.

Proverbs 22:6 (ESV)

IF YOU HAVE CHILDREN or grandchildren, you are probably keenly aware that they are very observant. (Trust me, they're watching and copying your every move.) And since children learn by example, wouldn't it be great if our children saw us enjoying happy, healthy, whole lives? Wouldn't it be awesome if our kiddos saw us making exercise a priority?

With approximately 25 percent of today's children falling into the "obese" category, we need to find fun ways to encourage fitness with the little ones we encounter because their healthy habits begin at home. Here are five family-friendly fitness ideas you could implement into your family's routine:

1) Scavenger Hunt

List ten things for your children to find, such as an acorn, a bird's feather, a dandelion, a mushroom, etc. Then, go into the woods and look for all of the items on the list, rewarding the winner of the scavenger hunt (the one who finds the most items) with the fun responsibility of choosing next week's family fitness activity.

If you don't live near a wooded area, you can have a "city scavenger hunt" by finding various urban items simply by pointing them out as you walk through the city as a family. For instance, you could have your children find a "yield" sign, a parking meter, a bus stop, etc.

2) Ultimate Frisbee Competition

Take your friendly Frisbee competition to a public park, and it might just turn into a massive competition with new friends and other families. Playing Frisbee involves running, jumping, diving, and throwing . . . great exercise and great fun! If you get enough people involved, you can even enjoy a fierce game of Frisbee football!

3) Family Fitness Challenges

Once a week, have a fitness contest and award a traveling trophy to the weekly winner. Then, let the winner keep the trophy in his or her room until the next fitness challenge. The kids will love this, and a little friendly competition is a good thing! Need some ideas for events?

a) King or Queen Cruncher: See who can do the most abdominal crunches in a minute.

b) Fabulous Flexibility Award: After stretching out, see who comes closest to touching his/her nose to the floor in a straddled position.

c) Push-up Champ: See who can do the most push-ups in sixty seconds.

d) Plank or Plop: Have everyone get into a plank position, and see who can hold their planking position the longest.

e) Top Jump Roper: See who can jump rope the longest without tripping or stopping.

4) Jump, Jump, Jump!

Speaking of jumping, how long has it been since you jumped rope? Not only is this activity a great workout, but your kids will get a kick out of seeing their parents jumping rope. Let your children teach you some of the jump-rope chants they know, and then teach them some chants from your playground past.

You can also practice counting and memorization while jumping rope. Here's some more incentive. A 155-pound person will burn approximately 372 calories for every 30 minutes of jumping rope. So, jump it up!

5) Walk and Talk

Even if your children are very young, not very athletically inclined, or too old to participate in the above fitness activities, they can walk alongside you.

Use your family walks to talk with your children about their hopes and dreams or pray with them about their concerns or fears. If they aren't feeling too talkative, use the time to impart wisdom, quote favorite movie lines to one another, make up stories together, etc.

You can also allow the younger kiddos to push their dolls in strollers. Oh, and don't forget Fido. He's a part of the family, too, right?

It's time we quit telling our kids to "*go* outside and play" and instead ask them to "*come* outside and play!" Whether you engage in some of the activities mentioned above or simply shoot some hoops with your children, you'll be making memories and burning calories. Your body and your children will thank you.

POWER PRAYER: *Father, I am thankful for the body You've given me, and I am asking that You help me in my endeavor to live a healthier lifestyle. And, Lord, please help me to set a good example for my children, encouraging them to be fit in every area of their lives—spiritually, physically, and mentally. In the Mighty Name of Your Son, Jesus, Amen.*

WORK YOUR WORDS: I will set a good example for the children in my life by making fitness fun and by making it a priority.

HEALTHY HINT: It's also a great idea to train as a family in preparation for a big race. Ally, my youngest daughter, and I trained and ran in the Downtown LA Turkey Trot a few years ago, and it was a blast! It was such a sense of accomplishment to cross the finish line right behind her.

CHAPTER 4

ENJOY THE JOURNEY

. . . .

*Look here, you who say, "Today or tomorrow we are
going to a certain town and will stay there a year.
We will do business there and make a profit." How do you
know what your life will be like tomorrow? Your life is like
the morning fog—it's here a little while, then it's gone.
What you ought to say is, "If the Lord wants us to, we will live
and do this or that." Otherwise you are boasting about
your own pretentious plans, and all such boasting is evil.*

James 4:13–16 (NLT)

I RECENTLY HEARD of a study involving the top CEOs of
the biggest companies in the world, and one common theme
was apparent. When interviewed, the majority of them said
something like this: "If I could do it all over again, I would
take time to stop and smell the roses. I would take more walks
with my spouse. I wouldn't be so stressed and uptight. I would
slow down and enjoy the journey more."

This intrigued me, as I am also very career-driven and
goal-oriented, so I researched this topic a bit more and

stumbled upon an article about Bronnie Ware, author of *The Top Five Regrets of the Dying: A Life Transformed by the Dearly Departing*. Ware, who cared for those who were nearing the end of their lives, wrote: "All of the men I nursed deeply regretted spending so much of their lives on the treadmill of a work existence."

After pondering, processing, and praying about all of this, I've come to this conclusion: Being driven is a good thing, as long as you take time to take care of yourself and enjoy the journey in all of your "driven-ness."

That's how we should live life.

We shouldn't be so consumed with our goals in life that we miss the privilege of living. It's important that we take time today and every day to appreciate the people and the blessings that God has given us. If we don't, when we finally reach our goals, after neglecting our friends and family along the way, we'll have no one to celebrate with us. Or we will have worked so hard and so long to accomplish our goals, that we'll be too tired or in too poor health to savor that success.

You know, I often hear people give the excuse, "If I had time, I'd exercise but I'm just too busy with work." My response is always the same, "Work will still be there tomorrow but if you don't take care of yourself, you may not be."

Okay, that may sound a little harsh, but it's true. No matter how driven we are in our careers or how busy we are chasing after our dreams, we have to make time for taking care of ourselves. That means you need to work in a workout on a consistent basis. It also means you should treat yourself to a massage and a pedicure once in a while. And it means you should make time to enjoy the loved ones in your life.

We really can have it all, if we do it God's way. Allow Him to prioritize your life and direct your steps. And don't be in so much of a hurry that you forget to bask in the beauty of the moment.

Every day is a gift, so treat it as such. Then, when we get to the end of our long, healthy lives, we won't have any regrets, only sweet memories of a life filled with love, laughter, success, and satisfaction.

Here are five things you should take time to do in the near future:

1. Read a book to a special child in your life.
2. Take ballroom dance lessons with your significant other. (It's fun and a great workout—get your foxtrot on!)
3. Watch the sun set, and thank God for painting the sky so beautifully.
4. Take your dog for a walk. (You'll have quality time with Fido and burn a few calories.)
5. Do something silly and fun with your family, like have a picnic in your living room or wear your pj's all day on Saturday while having a movie marathon.

POWER PRAYER: *Father, help me to take time for myself and enjoy this wonderful life that You've given me. Help me, Lord, to be able to set boundaries where work is concerned and better prioritize my life so I can enjoy some downtime. I love You. In the Mighty Name of Your Son, Jesus, Amen.*

WORK YOUR WORDS: I will take time to enjoy the journey on the way to achieving my goals.

HEALTHY HINT: Part of enjoying life is simply choosing not to rush through it! Space enough time between your future appointments so that you can make each one without going at a crazy, rushed pace. Also, purposely live in the moment today. When you're with your family, put away the cell phone and be present in every sense of the word.

CHAPTER 5

KEEP LOOKING FORWARD . . .

Let your eyes look directly forward,
and your gaze be straight before you.
Proverbs 4:25 (ESV)

JUST RECENTLY, I WAS listening to a podcast of Pastor Joel Osteen of Lakewood Church in Houston, Texas, and he said something that really grabbed my attention. He said, "You've got a big windshield on the front of your car. And you've got a little, bitty rearview mirror. The reason the windshield is so large and the rearview mirror is so small is because what has happened in your past is not nearly as important as what is in your future."

That's good, isn't it?

In other words, let the past be the past at last. The more we hang on to what's happened in the past, the harder it is to move forward with confidence, excitement, and determination. If someone hurt you in the past, forgive that person (even if you have to forgive by faith because you're not feeling it), and move on. Or, if you had a very troubled childhood, filled with more heartache than happiness, give it to God! Shake it off, and move forward. I realize, of course, that those things are easier said than done, but with God all things are possible. You can move forward, if you'll only stop looking back.

As I pondered the podcast's message, I realized it's not always the bad things in our past that we have to let go of in order to move on; sometimes, it's the really good things. This is especially true when it comes to the way many of us think about our bodies.

Women often speak in terms of their "PC bodies" (Pre-Children bodies) or their "college bods," referring to those seasons as the "good old days"—the days when they felt best about themselves in terms of overall appearance. But that kind of thinking can be crippling. Simply put, if you're in your forties, your goal shouldn't be to look like you did when you were twenty-two. Things change. Bodies age. Various body parts drop (and that kind of "dropping it low" isn't hot, lol). But that's okay. By adjusting our goals and stopping ourselves from yearning for the good old days—we shoot for a healthy, fitter version of the bodies we have today. That's not settling, that's just being realistic.

I have a friend who is well-known in the fitness industry, and she shared that one of her clients fell into this "longing for the good old days" mentality. Her client had a pair of jeans that she'd worn in college and had kept them for more than twenty-five years in hopes she would one day fit back into them. Finally, this lady in her midforties lost enough weight and trained hard enough that she actually slid into those Levi's and zipped them up comfortably. She was ecstatic! However, her elation was short-lived because she couldn't maintain that weight or size, no matter how hard she worked out or how healthy she ate. Finally my friend said to her frustrated client, "Did you ever think your body is trying to tell you something? Your set point is not what it was at twenty-two. You can maintain one size bigger without much effort and you look and feel amazing at that weight and size. Let's be happy with that accomplishment and stop fighting with your body."

Once her client heard that voice of reason, it was freeing to her. She no longer demanded her body to become what it was at twenty-two. Instead, she enjoyed life, looking and feeling great in a pair of jeans one size larger. And guess what? She could finally retire the "college jeans," which were out of style anyway. Yay!

So, let me ask you this: Is there something from your past that you need to release to God today, something that's holding you back? Or are you still longing for the good old days instead of living in the moment and looking forward to the future with anticipation? It's time to let go, and let God.

POWER PRAYER: *Father, help me to keep looking forward with You and stop yearning for what used to be. Help me, Lord, to let go of any hurt from the past and move forward in all that You have for me. In the Mighty Name of Your Son, Jesus, Amen.*

WORK YOUR WORDS: I choose to stop looking back and longing for what used to be. Instead, I will enjoy today and be excited about tomorrow in every area of my life, including the way I feel about my body.

HEALTHY HINT: If you're still hanging on to an old pair of college jeans in hopes you'll one day fit into them, get a new dream! Let the past be the past at last and reward yourself today for the strides you're currently making on the road to a healthier, happier version of yourself. For example, if you are finally able to jog two miles without stopping, buy yourself a couple of new workout tanks. (I just bought one for myself that says, "My game face includes mascara." haha! Love it!)

CHAPTER 6

WATCH YOUR WORDS

· ·

*Words kill, words give life; they're either
poison or fruit—you choose.*
Proverbs 18:21 (MSG)

I WAS ON MY FOURTH OUTFIT and totally disgusted with myself. As I looked into the mirror, focusing on my figure flaws, I sighed in defeat.

"I am so fat."

No matter how I turned my head, sucked the gut in, or positioned myself in front of the mirror, I could only see what was wrong with my body. I didn't focus on the definition of my arms from strength training. I didn't see that my jeans fit less snugly than they had just three weeks before due to recent weight loss. And I didn't notice that my butt looked a bit higher from all the squats and lunges I'd been doing at the gym. All I saw was a body that was bigger than it had been pre-children, and one that needed improvement.

After trying on yet another outfit, I looked into the mirror one last time and said, "I am so fat!" with a bit more emotion this time. I was so consumed with wallowing in self-loathing, that I hadn't noticed my oldest daughter, Abby, who was five at the time, coloring pictures on my bed.

The next morning, as my two daughters were putting on the outfits I had laid out for them the night before, Abby tilted her head, posed in front of the bathroom mirror, and said, "I'm so fat."

I was sure I hadn't heard her correctly.

"What did you say?"

"I'm fat," Abby said again.

Oh my gosh! What have I started? I thought.

"No, you're not, babe," I assured her. "You're perfect! You're beautiful!"

As I continued to reassure my sweet Abby that she was perfectly formed by Almighty God, I realized that my negative self-talk was no longer just affecting me, it was also affecting my children—and that wasn't okay. I wish I could tell you that I immediately changed my ways and never uttered another "I look fat in these jeans" kind of statement again, but I can't. It was a process. But I finally realized that saying, "I'm fat," all the time was poisoning my daughters' minds with wrong thinking, and it wasn't helping me, either. In fact, the more I heard myself say those words, the more I believed them.

You know, the Bible says that faith comes by hearing, and I was hearing myself say negative things about myself day after day and thus, building my faith in the wrong area. It wasn't until I changed my negative self-talk and began saying positive things about myself that my mind-set changed.

Let me give you a visual so you can understand this concept a little better. Let's say you have two dogs, and you feed one every single day, but you only give the other doggie a small morsel once a week. After several weeks, your two dogs get into a fight. Which dog do you think will win that doggie duel? Of course, the answer is obvious—the dog you've been feeding regularly will win the battle easily because he will be stronger.

So, let me ask you something . . . which dog have you been feeding? If you've been feeding the negative self-image Fido, that depressing doggie is sure to overpower your positive pup. Seriously, what have you been saying about yourself? When is the last time you looked in the mirror and said something nice?

You may be thinking: *But I don't look fine. I'm not going to lie to myself and say I look fit and fabulous when I don't.* And I'm not asking you to do that if you aren't comfortable with that morning mantra, but I am asking you to stop making negative comments about yourself and start looking for areas where you can make positive observations. For example, you may not be at your ideal weight at this very moment, but maybe you have been walking faithfully five times a week for the past three months and you've noticed a bit more definition in your thighs. So, instead of saying, "I'm twenty-five pounds heavier than I was before I had children," declare: "I can really see an improvement in the muscle tone of my legs since I began my walking program." It's a shift in your thinking, which will cause a shift in your speaking, and a shift in your speaking will cause a shift in your overall attitude. So, go ahead. Toot your own horn today and say, "Girl, you are looking better than ever!"

POWER PRAYER: *Father, help me to stop the negative self-talk and begin confessing good things over myself. Help me to see myself through Your eyes, Lord, and help me to celebrate my progress. I love You, God, and I'm so thankful that You love me. In the Mighty Name of Your Son, Jesus, Amen.*

WORK YOUR WORDS: I will stop saying ugly things about myself. Instead, I will say good things. In fact, I'll start now: "Girl, you are looking fine today!"

HEALTHY HINT: To celebrate and document your progress, why not take your measurements along the way? Your weight shouldn't be the only tool you use to measure your success. By taking your body measurements, you'll be able to see the number of inches you've lost, which is exciting to chart! There are great resources online and on YouTube that show you how to measure accurately.

CHAPTER 7

CHANGE YOUR MIND-SET

. . . .

For as he thinks in his heart, so is he.

Proverbs 23:7 (NKJV)

I HAVE A VERY CLOSE FRIEND who has struggled with her weight most of her adult life. She is absolutely stunning, but she had let her weight get out of control following the birth of her second child. She found herself more than seventy-five pounds past her ideal weight, which made her feel very depressed, unworthy, and unattractive. She had tried several fad diets only to end up regaining more weight than she had originally lost. It was a vicious cycle, and she was fed up. So she finally got up the nerve to go to a doctor about her situation, wondering if her hormones were off or if there was a medical condition that was preventing her from losing weight. This took a lot of courage because she was embarrassed of her weight, and she knew she'd have to get on the doctor's scales at her appointment. But she swallowed her pride and kept her appointment, even allowing the nurse to weigh her.

As she fidgeted in the small room awaiting the doctor, she contemplated leaving, but just as she was about to leave, Dr. Discouragement walked in.

He shook my friend's hand and then uttered these words, "So, how long have you been obese?"

Ugh.

Obese? Really! Don't you think he could've been a bit more sensitive and encouraging? Well, that appointment didn't do much for my friend's self-esteem, and she left there feeling more defeated than ever. Months later, after she'd licked her wounds for a bit, she made another appointment with a different doctor to see if he could help her get on an eating and exercise plan that would enable her to conquer her weight issue once and for all. Though she was nervous because of her previous experience with Dr. Discouragement, she arrived at the new doctor's office with one last shred of hope. As she sat in the small waiting room this time, she prayed that God would help her remove this seemingly impossible obstacle in her life. Just then, in walked Dr. Destiny. He took one look at my sweet friend and said, "Well, aren't you absolutely gorgeous?" (And she is!)

What a different start to the appointment, eh?

Then he proceeded to speak heartfelt words to her, assuring her that she could lose weight and get fit. He told her that it wasn't an impossible task, and then he said, "Even if you didn't lose a single pound, you'd still be beautiful. But I can tell from what you've shared with me that you would feel better physically, mentally, and emotionally if you lost weight, so do it for yourself. I'll do all I can to help."

And that was it.

She left his office feeling empowered, with a totally different mind-set, knowing that there wasn't anything physically keeping her from becoming a healthier, happier version of herself. Dr. Destiny didn't give her any magic potion to help her lose 30 pounds in 30 days. No, he didn't perform any weight-loss surgeries on her. Instead, he told her the amount of calories she needed to consume every day in order to keep her metabolism firing and working at an optimum level based on several factors (her age, current weight, body type, and daily activity level), and then he recommended that she eat five small meals a day. Lastly, he suggested that she walk two to three miles, three to four days a week. None of those suggestions seemed too difficult to follow, so she followed them and her weight decreased at a steady pace while her fitness level increased. She is almost at her goal weight now, and she continues to amaze me.

Do you see what a change in mind-set can accomplish? My friend went from wallowing to winning. So, what's your mind-set like today? Do you see yourself as a victim or a victor? Don't let your negative thoughts about yourself or what anyone else has said about you dominate your mind. Instead, think on this—you can do this! You can do all things through Christ Jesus!

Change your mentality, and you'll change your reality.

POWER PRAYER: *Father, I am asking You to change my mind-set. Help me to see myself as You see me, and help me to love myself the same way that You love me. With You, Lord, I believe that I can make the necessary changes I need to make in order to become a healthier, happier version of myself. In the Mighty Name of Your Son, Jesus, Amen.*

WORK YOUR WORDS: I am a victor, not a victim! With God, I am capable of transforming myself into a healthier, happier version of myself, and I am excited about it!

HEALTHY HINT: There are so many diet plans out there, that it's hard to know which one will work best for your body. Best advice? Do like my friend did and go to the doctor to make sure there's nothing physically keeping you from attaining your ideal body weight, and then ask your doctor to recommend an eating plan. "Diets" are temporal, but a change in eating habits is a lifetime adjustment that will equal lasting results.

CHAPTER 8

EXERCISE IS WORSHIP

. . . .

But the Lord said to Samuel, "Don't judge
by his appearance or height, for I have rejected him.
The Lord doesn't see things the way you see them.
People judge by outward appearance,
but the Lord looks at the heart."

1 Samuel 16:7 (NLT)

"IF YOU TRULY BELIEVE that your body is the temple of the Holy Spirit, you will be willing to make those lifestyle changes that will positively affect your health. We only get one body, and we need to take care of it. Increasing daily physical activity or beginning an exercise program won't seem so much like work if you're doing it unto the Lord."

I was interviewing exercise physiologist John Latham for an article I was writing for a health magazine, and when he said those words, it was life-changing for me. Up until that moment, exercise had always been a way for me to keep my weight down so that I could simply look good in my jeans, and if there were some health benefits, then yay! It was a bonus. Bottom line: My motives for movement were wrong. I truly had never thought of working out unto the Lord, but the more I pondered his words and studied and prayed, I began getting more revelation.

And here's my conclusion: Exercise really can be an act of worship unto God. Now, I know that may sound a little super-spiritual, but hear me out. Movement is from God. I believe He is the author of exercise because He is the author of everything good. There is life in exercise! Deuteronomy 30:19 says that "I have set before you life and death . . . choose life" (KJV). Well, that's what we're doing every time we choose to exercise instead of giving in to our flesh and finding reasons not to move.

As you walk, jog, run, do yoga, ride your bike, do pilates—whatever—commit that time to the Lord. Actually pray, *Lord, I commit this exercise time to You. I ask You to help me improve my health—both physically and spiritually. Speak to me, Lord, during these minutes. I love You.*

Here are some suggestions to get you started. Play some quiet worship music and stretch, working on flexibility, while sitting quietly in His presence. Or play some rocking Christian music and dance unto the Lord! Dancing is great exercise, and if David danced before the Lord, well . . . then so should we! Or, if you're really dealing with something, like spiritual battle kind of stuff, do some roundhouse kicks and kickbox that aggression and frustration right out of you. You might even say, "I'm kicking you out of my life, devil!" as you punch your way through your workout. Trust me; it's one of the most free-ing, exhilarating times you'll ever have in an exercise session.

Lastly, remember that as we get fit and strong and active and able to fulfill our destinies in Him, we glorify God through our bodies! Now, if that doesn't motivate you to move it, I don't know what will! I love how the *Message* version puts 1 Corinthians 6:20: "The physical part of you is not some piece of property belonging to the spiritual part of you. God owns the whole works. So let people see God in and through your body."

God owns the whole works! Let's honor Him in every area of our lives because He is so good to us! Now, put on those running shoes . . . your worship session awaits!

POWER PRAYER: *Father, help me to worship You through my workouts. Help me, Lord, to keep my heart pure and my priorities straight. Thank You, God, for the ability to move my body and participate in exercise. Help me, Lord, to bring glory to You in all that I do. I love You. In the Mighty Name of Your Son, Jesus, Amen.*

WORK YOUR WORDS: I will worship You, God, in my workouts. And I am grateful that I am able to exercise.

HEALTHY HINT: I am kind of a visual person, so it helps me to post notes and scriptures as reminders and encouragement. Maybe you're like that, too. If so, post notes like this: "Strive for Progress, not Perfection"; "I Worship You, Lord, through My Workouts"; and "I Am Strong and Active and Able to Be Used by God."

CHAPTER 9

WRITE THE VISION

. . . .

May he grant your heart's desires
and make all your plans succeed."
Psalm 20:4 (NLT)

WHEN I MENTOR other writers, I begin each mentorship by asking my clients to think through, pray about, and finally write down the five specific writing/publishing goals they have for our two months together. I do this for three reasons. First, I want them to write their goals and post them in a place where they will see them every day so they will be reminded and accountable. Second, I need to know their goals so that I can help them achieve those dreams. And, third, I ask them to do this because it's the way God does things. Habakkuk 2:2 tells of God's instruction: "Then the LORD answered me and said, 'Record the vision and inscribe it on tablets, that the one who reads it may run'" (NASB).

In other words, write down your goals; make them very plain and specific; and then run with those goals! Go for it! Achieve those dreams!

This "goal writing exercise" has proven very effective with my writing mentoring clients, and guess what? This same method also works well when it comes to our health and fitness goals. But simply writing them down isn't enough to make them come to pass. Studies have shown that there are three key components that indicate whether or not you will accomplish your goals. First, did you make a firm commitment? Second, were your goals realistic? And, third, did you keep track of your progress along the way and celebrate the victories?

So, let me ask you—can you answer yes to those three questions? If not, it's not too late. You can start today! (I'll help you!) Okay, first let's look at the definition of a "firm commitment." Basically, making a firm commitment means that you've thought about your goals, prayed about them, discussed them with your family and possibly your physician, and you have no doubt about what you wish to accomplish.

Second, let's look at what constitutes a realistic goal. (This one is super important!) You probably already know that a healthy and doable weight loss rate is about two pounds a week. Of course, the rate at which you will lose weight will depend on how much you have to lose, your diet, the amount of exercise you do, your age, etc. You might lose more than two pounds a week if you go on a crash diet, but more than likely, that weight will return if you don't make permanent lifestyle changes. Slow and steady is the way to go. With all of that understood, don't make an unrealistic goal such as, "I plan to lose thirty pounds in thirty days." When you make unrealistic goals, you set yourself up for failure and discouragement.

Lastly, it's crucial to record your progress. You can purchase a weight-loss/fitness journal just about anywhere. (I found one recently at the Dollar Tree!) Of course, you can use a basic notebook or your smartphone to track your daily eating and exercise habits. One of the tools that I love to use is an online program called My Fitness Pal (myfitnesspal.com), where you can keep track of your food intake and your calorie expenditure through exercise. Of course, there's an app for that program, perfect and convenient for your smartphone or tablet.

Now for the fun part of number three—the celebrating part! When you accomplish a goal, reward yourself! For example, if you train for a 5K and you run it successfully, reward yourself with a new pair of running shoes or a new workout tank. Or, maybe you are finally able to lose those twenty-five pounds that you thought were there to stay forever. Reward yourself with a new clothes shopping spree (in a new smaller size)! It's important to celebrate the small victories on the way to reaching your overall goals.

The experts didn't suggest this last tip, but I think it's just as important as the other three. Find scriptures that pertain to your goals, and write them out beside your goals. Then read those verses every day and stand on them as you push through to victory!

Once you've written down your goals and you've found

the corresponding scriptures, pray over them and share your vision with your family and your doctor. Now you're ready!

You can do this!

POWER PRAYER: *Father, help me determine the best weight-loss/fitness goals for my body and, Lord, help me to be realistic and specific as I set those goals. Lastly, Lord, help me to remain encouraged as I press toward victory in every area of my life. I love You. In the Mighty Name of Your Son, Jesus, Amen.*

WORK YOUR WORDS: I will go after my goals with passion, drive, wisdom, and heart. I can do all things with God.

HEALTHY HINT: When establishing your weight-loss and fitness goals, make sure they are not only realistic, but also specific. So, a goal such as "I plan to eat healthier" is too generic. A more specific goal would be, "I plan to cut out all soda, and drink at least 64 ounces of water every day."

CHAPTER 10

DON'T FEAR
THE LIGHT

· ·

*"This is the crisis we're in: God-light streamed into the world,
but men and women everywhere ran for the darkness.
They went for the darkness because they were
not really interested in pleasing God."*

John 3:19 (MSG)

SOMETIMES IN MY MIND I look better than I do in real life. Do you do that, too? Maybe it's a defense mechanism; I'm not sure. But when I see a cute workout outfit and I picture myself in it, I don't picture cellulite showing through the fabric or bulges of any kind. So when I take that cute workout outfit into the dressing room, I often get a shock.

And not in a good way.

What is it about that dressing room lighting? It's so *not* flattering! It truly reveals every bump, bulge, and imperfection, which usually leads to a dressing room meltdown.

Remember the dressing room scene in the movie *White Chicks* when one of the girls has a major meltdown? One

45

moment she is fine and then she tries on an outfit and goes a little crazy:

> Hi, I'm Cellulite Sally; look at my huge ba-donkey. Don't forget about me, I'm Backfat Betty. Now, who could have said that? Oh yeah, it's Tina the Talking Tummy," she says, crying hysterically. "I can't even wear a short skirt and a top without looking like a fat pig.

While that's hilarious in the movie, it's not so funny when you're the one having the meltdown. I speak from experience. But, seriously, there is something sort of unforgiving about that fluorescent lighting.

You know, light is a powerful thing. It reveals much about us, sometimes more than we care to know.

This is also true in spiritual matters.

The Bible says that Jesus is the Light of the World. When we look to Him and His Word, it also reveals much about us. Through His Word, you may find areas of darkness in your life that you weren't even aware existed. The Lord may shine His light on bitterness that's been hiding in a dark corner of your heart. Or the Lord may shine His light on that unforgiveness you've been harboring for years. Or He may shine his light on that anger you thought you'd dealt with, yet there it is, still lingering in your heart.

Looking into the Light of the Word of God can be a little

overwhelming. You'll most likely see some flaws in yourself that you didn't realize were there. But don't have a meltdown and run from Jesus and the Bible when you see your flaws and shortcomings. Instead, embrace the truth and ask the Lord to get rid of the flaws that He so graciously exposed, because He will! God heals what He reveals. God wants you to live free from that mess. He wants you to live life happy, healthy, and whole. That's why He has illuminated the situation for you. Finding out you have areas that need work is simply the first step toward breaking free of those strongholds. Let Jesus and His light fill you up and flow out of you. Continue to look into the Word and allow His light to reveal areas where you need growth. When you do, you'll find that you are being transformed.

As for that dressing room lighting, give yourself a break. Don't go off on a "Cellulite Sally" rant. Instead, appreciate the progress you've already made and own that body you've got. Look at yourself in that dressing room mirror and say, "Girl, you may not be perfect, but you are looking good."

POWER PRAYER: *Father, thank You for revealing those strongholds in my life that have kept me from truly living happy, healthy, and whole. I give my whole heart to You and ask that You heal those hurt places in my life so that I can fulfill my destiny and enjoy the journey while fulfilling it. In the Mighty Name of Your Son, Jesus, Amen.*

WORK YOUR WORDS: I will not fear any light, and I will walk in God's light today and always.

HEALTHY HINT: Speaking of light, sunlight is actually good for you—as long as you don't get too much. Here are some of its benefits: It's a germ killer, relaxer, sleep enhancer, and mood booster. So, get off the treadmill and actually venture outside for a twenty-minute walk today, and enjoy a little sunshine!

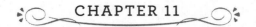
YOU ARE
WONDERFULLY MADE

. . . .

For you created my inmost being; you knit me
together in my mother's womb. I praise you because
I am fearfully and wonderfully made.

Psalm 139:13–14 (NIV)

ARE YOU JOYFUL TODAY? Are you celebrating the person God made you to be?

If you answered, "Not so much," we need to work on changing that answer to an absolute "Yes!" Because in order to enjoy this wellness journey and not become weary along the way, you are going to need that supernatural joy to keep you going. Especially on the day when you get a bad health diagnosis. Or on the day when you've been working hard at the gym and eating better and your weigh-in shows a two-pound increase. Or on the day when you give in to emotional eating and have an all-out binge. On those days, you can't look at the circumstances and be happy, but you can still be joyful knowing the following truths:

- You are a masterpiece! When God formed you, He was pleased, and He still is.
- God's love for you isn't based on your performance. God is a God of grace, and He loves you even when you mess up.
- You are a child of the Most High God. You don't have to earn His approval; you're already approved!
- The Scriptures say that God is changing us from the inside out, from glory to glory. That means you're in a stage of glory right now!

Meditate on all four of those truths for a moment or two and feel that joy rise up on the inside. See yourself as God sees you—in a stage of glory! When you are able to do that, you'll be able to accept yourself right where you are on the way to where you're going. In other words, you'll be able to love yourself—flaws and all—while you're in the process of changing.

I realize that this is easier said than done, but here's what I've discovered. If I am "me" focused, I have a very hard time keeping a joyful heart. Because when I am "me" focused, I dwell on all of my flaws (both spiritually and physically) and I have a hard time seeing myself through God's eyes. But when my heart is toward God and I'm focused on Him, my joy returns even if my circumstances remain the same. Because when my heart is toward God, I see everything from His perspective, and the issues and problems I have that seemed so huge all of a sudden seem quite small and easy to overcome. That shift in perspective makes all the difference in my joy level, and guess what? It will make a difference in your joy level, too.

Bottom line: If you keep your heart toward God, that's half the battle. Realize that God is the Potter; you are the clay; and you are in His hands. Let Him mold and shape you today, realizing that your lump of clay is pretty amazing throughout the entire process.

If you get nothing else from this book, I want you to get this—you're not a mistake. God doesn't make mistakes. You don't have to reach a certain weight to qualify for that whole "being perfectly created" verse. You already qualify!

You see, when you change your attitude and see yourself as God sees you, you'll feel better about yourself and you'll want to take care of yourself. You'll want to lose weight and get fit not for vain purposes, but to glorify God and increase your ability to fulfill your calling. So, be joyful today. You have every reason to be . . .

POWER PRAYER: *Father, thank You for creating me and loving me as You change me from glory to glory. Help me, Lord, to see myself as You see me and to walk this journey of wellness with joy in my heart. I love You, Lord. In the Mighty Name of Your Son, Jesus, Amen.*

WORK YOUR WORDS: I am wonderfully created by the Most High God, and I am being changed from glory to glory.

HEALTHY HINT: It's good to remind yourself that you were fearfully and wonderfully made. I have a plaque that hangs in my office as a reminder, but you don't have to invest in one of those unless you want to. You can just simply write those words on a Post-it Note and place it on the fridge or on your car's visor. Remind yourself often, and say it out loud!

CHAPTER 12

WORKING ON A TESTIMONY

. . . .

He reached down from on high and took hold of me;
he drew me out of deep waters. He rescued me from my
powerful enemy, from my foes, who were too strong for me.

Psalm 18:16–17 (NIV)

DRIVING HOME FROM her doctor's appointment that March day in 2000, Carol Layton couldn't help but notice the beauty of the season. Bright-colored flowers dotted the green hills as she drove down the highway. North Carolina was always pretty in the springtime. It would be a perfect day to take a hike in the woods with her grown children or walk around the block with her husband, but my friend couldn't do either of those things very easily—not at 340 pounds.

Even though Carol had been overweight most of her life, she hadn't been plagued with many health challenges, so when her mammogram showed "abnormalities" this time, Carol was devastated.

I've got to do something about this weight, she thought, knowing obesity was a risk factor for so many diseases.

It was the nudge she needed to get serious—one more time—about losing weight.

Carol charged into her home and headed straight for her closet. Rummaging through shoes, purses, and other stuff, she finally saw them—all of the Marty Copeland spiritual weight-loss products that Carol had ordered several months earlier.

This was it.

Carol opened the *Arise and Walk* video and popped it into her VCR.

Lord, I don't know if I am up for this, Carol prayed. *You're going to have to help me.*

As she listened to Marty share how God had set her free from the bondage of weight, Carol began to sob.

"I heard her testimony and I thought, *I want to have a testimony, too,*" Carol shared, reflecting. "I felt spiritually weak, and I wanted to get stronger in every area. I wanted to lose weight and keep it off. I wanted to get healthier."

Then Marty Copeland pointed at the camera and said, "Go out there and prove it!"

I will, Carol thought. *This time I will!*

Though she'd been dieting on and off since she was in the first grade, Carol knew that it would be different this time because she wasn't trying a new miracle diet; she was involving God in her eating in order to get free from the bondage of weight that had plagued her for so many years.

"I remember waking up one morning and feeling different," Carol shared with me. "I realized that I didn't have to wait until I reached my goal weight to get free and happy. I felt free and happy and I'd only lost ten pounds with more than a hundred left to lose! It was so different this time. Even after I attained my goal weight on previous diets, I was never free because I lived in fear of gaining back the weight."

She put a reminder Post-it Note on her fridge that said, "Prove it!"

And, boy did she ever!

Through God's power and grace, Carol lost 130 pounds and has had no more abnormal mammograms or any other health scares. She works out five days a week; sometimes leads a Christian yoga class at a local health club; and ministers to others struggling with weight and bondage.

"People are amazed when I say, 'I didn't go on a diet. I lost weight God's way,'" Carol shared. "I think the victory is even sweeter because God gets the glory!"

Her greatest test—the bondage of weight—has truly become her greatest testimony. When people ask how she lost so much weight and how she continues to maintain that weight loss, she is able to share her story.

How about you? Are you ready to share your story of victory? If God did it for my friend Carol, He will do it for you. After all, God is no respecter of persons, He is only a respecter of faith. When Carol finally quit trying to win the war with weight the world's way and surrendered the situation to God, she discovered freedom, success, and peace. God was waiting on her to involve Him in her battle from day one—all she had to do was ask. So, get your faith on, and start believing God for victory in this area of your life!

POWER PRAYER: *Father, I have tried and failed many times trying to lose weight and get fit the world's way, so I am asking today that You take the reins. I trust You, Lord, and I'm excited about the victory in store. In the Mighty Name of Your Son, Jesus, Amen.*

WORK YOUR WORDS: I will be like Carol and involve God in my wellness journey. I am working on a testimony, and I'm excited about it.

HEALTHY HINT: In order to lose over 100 pounds, Carol said this: "I started eating three healthy meals a day and a banana at 3:30 every afternoon. And I didn't indulge in everything that I wanted. I remember sowing self-control after getting home from work, making myself wait even one minute before eating dinner, just to practice the spiritual principle."

CHAPTER 13

GOD ADORES YOU

. . . .

*See how very much our Father loves us, for he calls us
his children, and that is what we are!*

1 John 3:1 (NLT)

EVERY TIME I WATCH the movie *What a Girl Wants* with
Amanda Bynes, I am moved to tears. She plays seventeen-year-
old Daphne Reynolds, and Colin Firth plays her estranged
dad. The scene that always gets me is when she is finally able
to dance with her father after longing to have a relationship
with him her entire life.

He tells her that he loves her and that he wouldn't change
a single thing about her as the song, "Have I Told You Lately
That I Love You?" plays in the background.

It's a lovely portrayal of that special relationship between
a father and daughter. I had that with my late father, Walter
Medlock, and I think because of that, I've never had a problem
understanding and accepting the love of my Heavenly Father.

Daddy used to tell me, "I've looked them all over, sweetie,
and you're the prettiest, sweetest, kindest, and smartest of them

all." (He told my siblings the same thing, haha, but I think he meant it more when he said it to me.) But you know what? I heard it so many times growing up, that his words built in me a confidence that made me think I could accomplish anything. I never once questioned my father's love for me.

But I realize not everyone grew up with a loving earthly father and may have never experienced that unconditional kind of love.

Whether you grew up with a stern dad who never said he loved you, an abusive father who only hurt you, or you've never even met your father, I have good news for you. Your Heavenly Father adores you, and He longs to have a close relationship with you.

In fact, the Bible says that He loves you with an everlasting love. Leviticus 26:12 further shows how much God wants a relationship with His children, when He says, "I will walk among you; I will be your God, and you will be my people" (NLT).

When you know God as your Father, you move from religion to relationship. He is no longer some distant deity in the sky or someone you've read stories about in an ancient book. No, when you truly know God, He becomes your Abba Father, which literally means "Daddy."

It's time we get to know our Heavenly Father better, and the only way to do that is to spend time in His presence—reading His Word, worshiping Him, and talking with Him.

If you don't know where to start, begin reading the Bible every day. But most importantly, spiritually crawl up into your Abba Father's lap and spend time with Him. Talk to Him and sit quietly in His presence so that He can talk to you. (I love doing this when I'm taking a walk, too!)

Once you accept your Heavenly Father's love, you'll be better able to love yourself, and that's a very important aspect in this whole "Love and Care for the One and Only You" concept. Because if you don't love yourself, then you won't have any desire to take care of yourself. You won't want to eat healthy or get fit because you don't think you deserve anything better than your current existence. But you do!

You may not feel worthy of love; therefore, you may have never even liked yourself, let alone loved yourself. But today is the day when all of that changes because you are worthy of love. God loves you! The Creator of the Universe adores you! He created you. And you didn't do anything to earn that love, therefore you don't have to do anything to keep it. He has loved you since before the foundations of the earth, and His love will continue throughout the ages. All you have to do is receive it.

Meditate on His goodness and the promises in His Word. And get to know your Heavenly Father. He'd love the chance to love on you today . . .

POWER PRAYER: *Father, thank You for loving me as only You can. Help me, Lord, to love myself more and accept Your love more easily. I understand in my head that You love me unconditionally, Lord. Help me to "get it" in my heart too. I love You. In the Mighty Name of Your Son, Jesus, Amen.*

WORK YOUR WORDS: I am loved by Almighty God, Creator of the Universe. In fact, He adores me!

HEALTHY HINT: In order to believe that God loves you with an everlasting love, you need to get that truth down on the inside of you. Try writing the following out on note cards and reading them aloud every day:

- He loves us so much that, He has engraved us upon the palms of His hand (see Isaiah 49:16).
- He loves us so much that, He will never leave us or forsake us (see Hebrews 13:5).
- He loves us so much that, the mountains shall depart, and the hills be removed; but my [Love] shall not depart from thee, neither shall the covenant of my peace be removed, saith the LORD that hath mercy on thee (see Isaiah 54:10, KJV).

CHAPTER 14

DON'T MISS OUT

·   •

So humble yourselves under the mighty power of God,
and at the right time he will lift you up in honor.
Give all your worries and cares to God,
for he cares about you.

1 Peter 5:6–7 (NLT)

HOW LONG HAS IT BEEN since you really liked yourself? Are you constantly pointing out your flaws, dwelling on your shortcomings, and wishing you were someone else? Have you avoided social engagements, charitable commitments, family get-togethers, class reunions, dates, vacations, and other activities simply because you didn't feel good about yourself? If you answered yes to any of those questions, you're not alone.

Even though, as women, we're more educated and empowered today than at any other time in history, it seems we can still be sidelined by a bad hair day. In fact, a Dove Self-Esteem ten-country survey revealed that two-thirds of females ages 15 to 64 admitted they would avoid normal activities if they felt badly about themselves.

Here is the breakdown of that study.

Worldwide, one in four women said she had passed on a social event; one in five had shunned physical activity; 18 percent said they had avoided joining a club; and 29 percent said they didn't go to the beach, spa, or swimming pool because they had experienced discomfort with their looks. What's more, 16 percent of those surveyed said they had even forgone a job interview because of a "bad hair day."

"The extent to which girls and women are changing their lives to accommodate how they feel about themselves is really alarming," wrote Sharon MacLeod, spokesperson for the Dove Self-Esteem Fund.

Be honest . . . you've avoided one or all of those things mentioned in the survey, haven't you? I think we all have, or at the very least, we've all wanted to skip an event because we felt less than attractive.

My five-year high school reunion would be one of those events. Okay, that was almost twenty-five years ago, but I still remember those months leading up to the all-important reunion. I had graduated from college with a journalism degree, married my high school sweetheart, and landed a job working for a daily newspaper. I was at a good place in my life, and I was looking forward to facing my former classmates. Months earlier, I had dreamed of walking into the reunion, looking thinner and prettier than I ever had in high school.

There was just one problem—I was pregnant with our first child. And I wasn't the "Oh, you're so pretty" pregnant type. I was the "Oh my goodness, when were you due?" kind of pregnant. I was huge! My face was swollen. My feet looked like Miss Piggy's hooves, and I was miserable. Plus, have you ever tried to find a really lovely maternity dress—one that is slimming, trendy, and doesn't scream "matronly" when you walk into a room?

Well, it isn't an easy task, and after trying on a coral pantsuit that made me look like a large, round piece of tropical fruit, I decided I would skip the reunion altogether. So that's what I did. I missed out on all of the fun because I was too worried about how ugly I'd look.

Pretty silly, huh? And, you know what else? I found out later that several other girls from my high school class were also big and pregnant at the reunion. I wouldn't have been the only one in the room with ankles the size of Texas. We could've traded pregnancy stories and bonded over baby stuff, but my fear of disapproval kept me from a wonderful night. And, truthfully, that same fear has kept me from enjoying many other wonderful times over the course of my life, as well. You might say I was a "Fearful Fran," scared of being judged and falling short.

Thankfully, that's not the end of the story. I've grown older and wiser, and I finally got tired of living in fear and missing out on life, so I asked the Lord to fill me up with His love so that there would be no room for fear.

First John 4:18 says, "There is no fear in love; but perfect love casts out fear . . ." (NKJV).

And that's exactly what the Lord has done for me. He will do the same for you.

I don't know what you've been missing out on because of your insecurities or what you've been avoiding due to a fear of rejection, but it's time to start living again. It's time to enjoy life! It's time to feel good about who we are! It's time to stop worrying about falling short and start walking tall!

It's time!

POWER PRAYER: *Father, help me to start living again and start loving myself. Help me, Lord, to let go of my insecurities and fears and allow You to fill me up with Your love and power. Help me, God, to be the person You intended me to be. I love You. In the Mighty Name of Your Son, Jesus, Amen.*

WORK YOUR WORDS: I will no longer allow fear to stop me from living. I am a child of the Most High God, and I am awesome because He is awesome!

HEALTHY HINT: Many times we are more susceptible to feeling badly about ourselves when we are sleep deprived or lacking in certain vitamins and minerals. It's always a good idea to get eight hours of sleep each night, as well as take a daily multivitamin. Also, when you start going down that negative road, stop yourself and make a list of the things in your life that you're proud of. For example, you may not have a 25-inch waist, but you're a really great mom who can throw an amazing theme party for your child's birthday. Focus on the positives!

CARDIO

CHAPTER 15

COME AS YOU ARE

. . . .

Come to me, all who labor and are heavy laden,
and I will give you rest.
Matthew 11:28 (ESV)

IT WAS THE MOMENT. I finally got up my nerve to ask her.

"So, would you want to come to church with us sometime? We'd love to have you."

She didn't even look up from the dessert we were sharing as she said, "I don't think I'm ready to go to church. I mean, I'm a mess . . . give me a few months to try and straighten out my life and ask me again."

Her response made me so sad. Though I tried to explain that you don't have to "straighten out" your life in order to come to church, but rather that's why we all go to church—to get straightened out—she still declined my invitation.

I wonder how many people feel the same way? I wonder how many people think they are a "mess" so they avoid the one place where they could find help, peace, fellowship, and faith?

Our church's senior pastor, Pastor Travis Inman, recently said, "The church is like a hospital for the sick. . . . If you're perfect, then don't come here, because we're liable to mess you up. We're not perfect, but we're perfectly loved by God."

That's good, isn't it?

Jesus said, "Come as you are!"

You know, the gym is the same way. The people who need it the most are often the ones who avoid it the most with excuses like, "Well, let me lose a few pounds first, and then I'll join." Or, "I'm a mess right now. I don't want to work out around all those perfect people." Yet the imperfect, out-of-shape, overweight people are the ones who need to be in the gym right now.

Do you avoid the gym because you feel less than perfect or you're intimidated by the gym rats who pose in the mirrors and make grunting noises? Well, it's time to swallow that pride, put on your running shoes, and head for the gym. You can't worry about what others think or how they view you. This isn't about them; it's about you! It's about your goals! It's about your health! And it's about time!

Listen, we all start somewhere, and it's not a competition. We aren't trying to compete with the twenty-year-old model who is training for an upcoming bikini shoot. We are simply trying to become a fitter, happier, healthier version of ourselves, right?

So, whether we're talking about church or the gym— "Come as you are" should be your mantra.

Don't worry about others looking down on you; just keep your eyes on your goals. Also, make an appointment with a personal trainer at your gym and ask if he/she could put together a routine specifically for you. Usually when you join a gym, a trainer will take you through the facility and show you how to use each piece of equipment—so ask about that tour. And be sure to check out the various classes. Whether you love to dance away the calories through Zumba or you'd rather do a cardio circuit class, your gym probably offers a wide variety of classes for various preferences and fitness levels.

So come as you are! No, seriously, get your gym clothes on, grab your water bottle, and go! Getting out the door is half the battle, so just do it. And remember, I'm cheering you on, and we're all on this health journey together. Proud of you! ☺

POWER PRAYER: *Father, help me to focus on You and my health goals and worry less about what others think of me. Give me courage, God, to push past my fears and insecurities and continue this journey of health. In the Mighty Name of Your Son, Jesus, Amen.*

WORK YOUR WORDS: I will not be intimidated! I will not worry about what others think. I will stay focused on my spiritual and physical goals.

HEALTHY HINT: Though you shouldn't stay away from the gym because of insecurities, there will be times when you simply can't get to the gym. For those days, you can follow YouTube or DVD workouts at home or in the privacy of your hotel room if you're traveling. One of my favorites to follow? Cassey Ho—the Blogilates chick. She offers YouTube workouts to sculpt and tone every body part, as well as fat-blasting cardio routines. Also, if you just want to do a quick workout that's effective, you can download various apps on your smartphone to guide you through various exercises. I love the 7 Minute Workout and the Nike Training app. They offer various workouts that will keep your exercise sessions exciting and fresh.

CHAPTER 16

FIND TIME FOR FITNESS

. . . .

But I trust in you, O LORD; I say, "You are my God."
My times are in your hands . . .

Psalm 31:14–15a (NIV)

YOU RISE BEFORE DAYLIGHT; spend a few minutes with God; get the kids up for school; pack their lunches; slurp down a glass of OJ while showering; get dressed; brush your teeth; make sure the kids get on the bus; do the nine-to-five thing; pick up the dry cleaning; go to the grocery store; rush home and fix dinner; help the kids with their homework; do a load of laundry; have at least one meaningful conversation with your spouse; look over your notes for tomorrow's meeting; call your mother; watch one of your DVR'd shows; and collapse into bed.

Sound familiar?

Life is busy, even if you don't work outside the home. That's why the number-one excuse for not exercising regularly is: "I just don't have time." But, guess what? There is time— even in your busy schedule. You just have to find it. Here are three practical ways to work exercise into your already jam-packed life.

1) Plan Ahead.

You have to approach exercise as if it's a meeting or a commitment you can't get out of. So take out your planner or tap on your smartphone's calendar, and look for open time slots. Then, start penciling in or typing in "exercise." That's a start! If it's on your calendar, you'll be more likely to do it.

2) Turn Off the TV.

According to recent data from Nielsen, adults from thirty-five to forty-nine years of age watch more than thirty-three hours of TV per week, and as we get older, our time in front of the TV increases! So, use part of your designated TV time to get fit. Hop on your bike and ride to the park, or call a friend and meet up at the local track for a nightly walk-and-talk session.

If you just can't miss your favorite programs, don't cuddle up in your comfy chair with a bag of chips. Instead, get on a treadmill or an exercise bike and sweat away the minutes of your favorite sitcom. The time will go faster if you're watching a show you enjoy, and before you know it, you will have completed thirty minutes of aerobic exercise.

Another fun way to use your TV time to get fit is this—do jumping jacks or jump rope or jog in place during all of the commercials.

3) Park Far Away; Take the Stairs.

Instead of circling the grocery store parking lot, searching for that parking space nearest the store, park in the very back of the lot. This will force you to walk at least three to five minutes to and from the store.

Or instead of taking the elevator at work or your apartment, take the stairs. Also, every hour or so at work—especially if you have a sedentary job—get up and walk around your department for a few minutes.

A few minutes here and a few minutes there are better than no minutes at all, and they add up. In other words, you don't have to do thirty *consecutive* minutes of aerobic exercise to enjoy the benefits. Most fitness experts agree that your body doesn't know the difference—so find ways to add minutes of aerobic activity to your daily routine.

Seem impossible? It's not. You can do it. Ask God to help you find time for fitness. He wants you to have a healthy body, so find time for exercise and honor the Father! As my pastor recently reminded us, you can't even spell God without "Go." So, get motivated and get GOing. Your healthy, fit body awaits . . .

POWER PRAYER: *Father, I give my day to You and all that is in it. Please, Lord, prioritize my "to-do" list and help me to find time to work in a workout. In the Mighty Name of Your Son, Jesus, Amen.*

WORK YOUR WORDS: I will let God prioritize my "to-do" list, and I will find time to work out today!

HEALTHY HINT: A great way to keep track of your fitness efforts is with a pedometer or one of the new exercise trackers like Fitbit. Some people find keeping track of their steps much easier than keeping track of their aerobic minutes throughout the day. Shoot for 10,000 steps each day!

CHAPTER 17

BONUS POINTS

. . . .

For I say, through the grace given unto me, to every man
that is among you, not to think of himself more highly
than he ought to think; but to think soberly, according
as God hath dealt to every man the measure of faith.

Romans 12:3 (KJV)

I'VE PRETTY MUCH TRIED every eating program known to man. Usually, I get talked into starting a new diet plan by a relative who doesn't want to go the diet journey alone. That's exactly what happened a few years ago when my niece, Autumn, called and asked me to go to a weight-loss meeting with her. She explained that the group met every Thursday in a church basement in our hometown. Wanting to drop a few pounds that I'd gained over the holidays (stupid Christmas cookies), I agreed to go and met her at the church where weigh-ins were already underway. After stripping down to the bare minimum (the most I could take off without being arrested) and getting weighed in, we sat down in the next room to learn the particulars of this very popular diet program.

I discovered the amount of points I could eat in one day and how many floater points I had available for the entire week. Next, we discussed high-point meals versus low-point options. I took notes and realized quickly how much I already despised this program. First, I would have to restrict my eating *a lot*, and I'd also have to do math—two of my least favorite things. Nevertheless, I embarked on this point-driven plan the following Monday. But by day four, I desperately desired my favorite sugary cereal for breakfast (Can anyone say Cinnamon Toast Crunch?), so I allowed myself to have it. After devouring every single sugary bite, I did the math. Yikes! I had consumed more than two-thirds of my daily allotted points in one meal!

Not good.

By two that afternoon, I was totally out of points and there were many hours remaining before bedtime. By 8 p.m., I was ravenous. In fact, I wanted to eat the notebook I was recording my points in, so I began complaining to my husband about my lack of points. He smiled his most mischievous smile and teased, "You can borrow some of my points." Real funny, eh? If I'd had enough strength, I would've throttled him, but I was too weak with hunger to react. So, I called one of my best friends in Texas who was a pro at the whole point thingy, and she had a good giggle over my diet dilemma too. But she was also the bearer of good news. She informed me that I actually had a few more points than I realized because I had failed to figure in my activity points for the day. Whoo-hoo! That was good to know. I was able to eat a handful of grapes and a few crackers before bed and still stay within my points for that day. I still went to bed rather hungry that night and vowed to use my points more wisely in the future.

Guess what? It's the same way in the spiritual realm. Unfortunately, we can't borrow spiritual points from our spouses, or anyone else for that matter. It would be so much easier to rely on my husband, Jeff, for everything—including extra eating plan points when I've used all of mine—but it just doesn't work that way. As much as he loves me, Jeff can't hear from God for me. He can't read the Bible for me. He can't do the things for me that I need to do to in order to grow in the Lord any more than he can give me his eating plan points and expect me to lose weight. At some point, we have to grow up and take responsibility for our own lives, doing what we know to do even when it's uncomfortable, inconvenient, or difficult. We can respect our loved ones and their faith, but we can't borrow it.

So, do the "do's" and grow up spiritually! Oh, and while you're at it, enjoy three Jolly Ranchers. They'll only cost you one point!

POWER PRAYER: *Father, help me to find the best eating plan for me, and please direct my steps as I educate myself in the eating and exercise realms. Also, help me to grow up spiritually, Lord. Thank You for loving me. In the Mighty Name of Your Son, Jesus, Amen.*

WORK YOUR WORDS: I will exercise regularly and eat a balanced, healthy diet so that I can achieve my fitness goals in a timely manner. I will also grow up spiritually on a healthy diet of God's Word.

HEALTHY HINT: When you're trying to lose weight through diet and exercise, it's important to remember that they go hand in hand, though studies have proven that what you eat is more important than the exercise component. In order to lose weight, the breakdown is generally 75 percent diet and 25 percent exercise, according to Shawn M. Talbott, PhD, nutritional biochemist and former director of the University of Utah Nutrition Clinic. "You can't out-exercise a bad diet," Talbott said in an article that appeared in a *Huffington Post* article called, "Exercise vs. Diet: The Truth About Weight Loss."

CHAPTER 18

DO THE "DO'S"!

. . . .

*"But we all, with unveiled face, beholding as in a mirror
the glory of the Lord, are being transformed into the same image
from glory to glory, just as by the Spirit of the Lord.*
2 Corinthians 3:18 (NKJV)

OVER THE COURSE OF a few days, I stumbled across three different inspirational quotations—all inspiring, all related, and all just for me. The first said, "Do something today that your future self will thank you for." The second said, "It's easier to take a small action now instead of a big action 'someday.'" And the third said, "What you do every day matters more than what you do every once in a while."

As I read the last one, which was on a bumper sticker on the car in front of me, I had to smile. I actually said out loud, "Okay, God, I get the message." What you don't know is that I had been planning on beginning a very restrictive diet plan on the following Monday. Truth be known, I had planned to start that popular diet program every Monday for the past month but it just never seemed like the right time. The thought of going on such a strict eating program with lots of rules and limitations had kept me from ever starting, even though several of my friends were having great success with it.

The message God was trying to communicate to me was simple: "You don't have to worry about all the 'can't haves' and 'don'ts' in your diet if you'll simply just implement the 'do's' on a daily basis. Doing the 'do's' will create healthy habits in your life and you won't have to do the restrictive plan you've been dreading for a month."

Here's what I've learned since that initial revelation from the Master Nutritionist. Good nutrition is just like anything else—we attain it in phases, "from glory to glory." So, don't be discouraged if you haven't eaten a vegetable in ten years (No, McDonald's french fries don't count . . .). If you replace a chocolate muffin with a piece of fruit today, you're one step closer to good nutrition. If you drink two glasses of water today and only one soda, you're one step closer to a healthier lifestyle.

Begin today implementing some healthy "do's" and the "don'ts" will start to take care of themselves.

It's the same way in our spiritual lives, really. New Christians, and even seasoned believers, often struggle with all of the "don'ts" and become discouraged in their Christian walk instead of doing what they know to do every day: read the Word of God, pray, praise, tithe, etc. All of the "thou shall not's" will take care of themselves as we grow closer to God by doing the "do's."

So, begin doing the "do's" in every area of your life today, and trust God to finish the good work that He has already begun.

Here are a few nutritional "do's" to get you started:

- **Replace eggs with egg whites.** Eggbeaters are great, and they have several varieties, including Southwest. This will cut your cholesterol considerably and still taste great! For a more festive omelet, add some peppers, mushrooms, turkey sausage crumbles, low-fat cheese, and picante sauce.
- **Drink at least 64 ounces of water each day**, and if possible, drink purified water instead of tap. Add some lemon or lime slices to "jazz it up" if you can't stomach straight water.
- **Use olive oil when cooking** (instead of other unhealthier options), and olive oil even comes in cooking spray now—yay!

POWER PRAYER: *Father, help me to do the "do's" every day in every area of my life. And help me, Lord, to begin craving healthy food and implementing healthy habits in my life so that I'll be fit both spiritually and physically. In the Mighty Name of Your Son, Jesus, Amen.*

WORK YOUR WORDS: I will do the "do's" today and every day from now on.

HEALTHY HINT: Want more healthy "do's" to add to your daily life?

Here are three more:

1. Change your white bread for whole grain bread (or even try Ezekiel bread, which you can find at most health-food stores now).
2. Eat three pieces of fruit every day.
3. Add cinnamon to your coffee or hot tea, because it has many health benefits.

CHAPTER 19

GET A FITNESS FRIEND!

*For where two or three are gathered in my name,
there am I among them.*

Matthew 18:20 (ESV)

CALL HER A "FITNESS FRIEND," a "Power Partner-in-crime," a "Power Pal," a "Workout Wingwoman," or a "Boot Camp Buddy." It doesn't matter what you call her, as long as you call her . . . or at least answer the phone when she calls you.

A Fitness Friend can play a huge part in your overall success of becoming a healthier, happier you. At least, that's been my experience as someone who never gets up in the morning and says, "Wow, I just can't wait to work out!"

Maybe you're like me, and if you are, then a Fitness Friend just might serve as the "GPS Prompter" you've been needing to put you on the path to a healthier version of you, and *keep* you on that path.

My youngest daughter, Allyson, is that GPS Prompter in

my life. We started working out together in 2011 in order to get ready for a spring break trip to Panama City Beach that would involve bathing suits . . . yikes!

If I said, "I'm too tired today," she would say, "Too bad. You'll feel better once you hit the elliptical." If I said, "Let's just go later . . . I have too much to do right now," she'd say, "Mom, get your workout clothes on and get in the car."

She wouldn't take no for an answer. She was determined to travel that path to a healthier, happier version of herself, and she had decided that she was going to take me along with her—even if she had to drag me kicking and screaming.

This went on three to five days a week for about four months. And after a few months, she didn't have to pull me down that path anymore. I went willingly. In fact, there were even days when I became the GPS Prompter in her life, texting her to meet me at the track.

My thinking had shifted somewhere along my "get healthier" journey. If I skipped a day or two at the gym, I missed it a little. That surprised me about myself. I had finally become consistent with my exercise routine long enough to experience its many benefits—sleeping better at night, fitting into my favorite jeans, feeling stronger, etc. Always before, I would do well for a few weeks, and then pull off "Healthy Highway" and take an extended rest at "I Really Don't Care Anymore Rest Stop."

Then I would get back up on "Healthy Highway" and start all over again . . . until I saw the exit for "I Really Hate

Working Out and I'm Way Too Busy Anyway Rest Stop," and I'd get off-course again.

What made the difference this time? I had my GPS Prompter, Allyson, to keep me on track. Together, we met our initial personal fitness goals and we continue to help each other stay on Healthy Highway even today, though I've made a few detours over the years. (My favorite exits are: "Powdered Donut Pathway" and "Butterfinger Boulevard.")

You know, you can apply this same principle to your spiritual life, as well.

Maybe you already have!

Do you have a prayer partner or a Bible study buddy? If not, maybe it's time you find one. I've had several over the years, but my very first prayer partner, Susan, actually taught me how to pray more effectively. Before Susan, I used to pray a few minutes during my morning devotional time and again at the end the day. And if something happened in between, I'd send up a few short prayers to God. But I hadn't ever committed to that concentrated, turn-the-cell-phone-off prayer time . . . until Susan.

By being my prayer partner, Susan had prompted me to take my prayer life to another level and become more spiritually fit, much like Allyson had prompted me to continue down Healthy Highway and become more physically fit.

We need each other.

If you need a prayer partner or even a fitness friend, God will send you one. Just ask Him. Or I could send you Allyson.

POWER PRAYER: *Father, thank You for loving me even when I take detours that aren't Your perfect path for my life. You are my heavenly GPS and I love You so much. Help me, Lord, to stay on the road to good health in every area of my life. In the Mighty Name of Your Son, Jesus, Amen.*

WORK YOUR WORDS: I am committed to becoming fit—spiritually and physically.

HEALTHY HINT: If you attend a women's Bible study, Sunday school, or a MOPS group, you can probably find your prayer partner and your fitness friend there. Who knows? She might even be the same person!

CHAPTER 20

YOU'RE ALMOST THERE . . .

. . . .

"But you, be strong and do not lose courage,
for there is reward for your work."

2 Chronicles 15:7 (NASB)

ALLYSON, MY TWENTY-YEAR-OLD daughter, and I were very excited to hike Runyon Canyon in LA. So many people had told us that it was a "must do," so we were pumped about finally getting the chance to do it; however, we didn't realize there were several different courses to take to the top, and we somehow ended up on the more advanced trail.

Scary.

Ally, who is twenty-five years younger than I am and in very good shape, was even huffing and puffing a little as we made our way up the steep inclines. I had gone way past huffing and puffing. If I could have caught my breath, I would have told Ally that I wanted to stop and rest for a bit, but I didn't have enough energy or air to try to holler for her as she hiked ahead.

I felt as though the hikers who passed by on their way down were secretly mocking me, and I was too proud to give up before reaching the top. I wanted to take that all-important Runyon Canyon selfie, documenting the fact that I had actually completed the hike—and on the advanced trail at that!

Still, as the sun beat down, I wanted to give up. Just then, I made eye contact with one of those hikers on the way back down the trail. She must have sensed my desperation because she smiled and encouraged, "You're almost there!"

With that piece of needed information, I had hope once again, so I put one Nike in front of the other and pressed on. Turns out, that helpful hiker was correct—I was almost to the top. I just didn't know it. I was able to finish and arrive at my destination just moments later. Honestly, if she hadn't shared that important tidbit of information, I might have quit just shy of my goal. I would've missed out on that feeling of accomplishment, and I never would've had the chance to take the celebratory Runyon Canyon selfie. Most importantly, I would have missed out on sharing that magical moment with my daughter.

That experience made me wonder how many times in life I had quit right before my breakthrough. I wondered how many times I might've missed out on something amazing because I threw in the towel too soon. How about you? Have you also been guilty of quitting when circumstances aren't ideal or when a situation gets too tough?

Apparently we are not alone. Minister of the gospel and

sports enthusiast, Chip Brim, shared a vision that God had given him. The Lord showed him thousands of Christians running down the football field. They started off strong, running with all of their might, striving toward their goal. But when they reached the one-yard line, they fell to the ground. Not one of them made it across the goal line to score the all-important touchdown. Instead, they all perished right there—one yard from their destiny.

Chip asked the Lord, "Why? What happened?" God told him, "They gave up too soon. They threw in the towel. They didn't know how close they were . . . "

So, my friends, if you've fallen down on the one-yard line—get back up. Ask God to help you. He will do His part if you'll do yours. Just don't give up. Keep pressing toward your goals! Because here's the good news—you're almost there!

POWER PRAYER: *Father, help me to stay on course and remain encouraged so that I don't quit—no matter how hard it gets. Thank You, Lord, for equipping me with everything I need—spiritually and physically—to finish well. In the Mighty Name of Your Son, Jesus, Amen.*

WORK YOUR WORDS: I am not a quitter! I will not give up! I will reach my goals!

HEALTHY HINT: If you've been walking inside on your treadmill or always walking the same few blocks in your neighborhood, why not change up your workout and go hiking? Not sure where to go? A quick internet search can assist you in finding a great new place to hike.

CHAPTER 21

JUST A CLOSER WALK

. . . .

For we walk by faith, not by sight.
2 Corinthians 5:7 (NKJV)

MAYBE YOU'RE NOT INTO the health club scene. Maybe you feel too uncoordinated to participate in an aerobic-dance class. Or maybe you're the outdoorsy type who can't stand spending an hour inside doing an exercise DVD or riding a stationary bike. Well, if you fit into any of these categories, then fitness walking is the perfect solution for you.

I love putting on my hot pink walking shoes and hitting the Milwaukee Trail, which is a popular fitness trail in my hometown, and I'm not alone. Walking is by far the most popular form of exercise, and it's one of the best and most convenient fitness activities around. You don't have to invest in an expensive piece of equipment. You don't have to join a gym. And you don't have to read a book, hire a trainer, or watch an instructor to know how to do it. Just slip on a good pair of walking shoes, and put one foot in front of the other!

Oh sure, there are a few things to know, but basically,

if you can walk, you can get an aerobic workout. Isn't that good news? Here's more good news. Walking, though it seems pretty easy when compared to other aerobic activities, has many health benefits. Studies show that walking briskly on a regular basis can lower your resting heart rate, reduce your blood pressure, lower your bad cholesterol, and increase the efficiency of your heart and lungs.

Walking not only has many health benefits, but it also has several spiritual benefits. It's true! Walking is an ideal way to spend time alone with the Father, giving Him your full attention. You'd be surprised how much prayer you can get in while pounding the pavement.

Use your daily fitness walk to pray for the people on the prayer list at church, your pastors, your unsaved family members and friends, and those in leadership on a local, state, national, and world level. Some days, you may just want to spend the entire walking time praising God for His goodness and mercy, which endure forever! Meditate on His goodness and thank Him for all that He is doing and has already done in your life.

You can also spend your walking time memorizing scripture, or listening to inspiring messages or an audio version of the Bible by simply plugging a pair of headphones into your smartphone. Get revelation as you walk your way to health and spiritual fitness. Feed your spirit as you reduce your body fat. It's a one-two punch to the devil!

Last, you can use your walking time to minister to your family. Take your children (or grandchildren) along on your walk, and find out what's going on in each of their lives. As you log the miles, you'll learn so much about your loved ones. Then, take the cool-down lap to pray over each concern that your children just shared with you. Your relationship with your family will become stronger, and most importantly, your relationship with God will grow stronger. Enjoy a closer walk with the Father as you walk your way to fitness. It's a journey worth making!

POWER PRAYER: *Father, thank You for loving me and desiring a relationship with me. Help me find time in my schedule to go on fitness walks with You. I am excited to share those walks with You, God. I look forward to our time together. In the Mighty Name of Your Son, Jesus, Amen.*

WORK YOUR WORDS: I will find time in my schedule to fit in a fitness walk, and I will use that time to improve my spiritual walk, as well.

HEALTHY HINT: To begin a walking program, you should:

- Invest in a good pair of walking shoes and wear them on every fitness walk.
- Wear comfortable clothing for your workouts—brightly colored if you walk at night.
- Try to walk at least twenty minutes at a steady pace three times a week, and increase your workout time, intensity, and frequency as your fitness level improves.
- Choose different routes so you won't get bored with your walking workout. (Another tip for fighting boredom? Listen to upbeat music.)
- Have fun! Walk with friends, family, and Fido! Get fit together!

CHAPTER 22

DON'T BE PEANUT BUTTER & JEALOUS

. . . .

*Do nothing from selfish ambition or conceit, but in humility
count others more significant than yourselves.*

Philippians 2:3 (ESV)

EVER SEEN THE TV COMMERCIAL promoting a particular weight-loss supplement where the husband and wife go on diets together and she hardly slims down at all, while he loses so much weight that his pants fall down? The goal of the commercial is to get women to buy a nutritional supplement that is made specifically to aid women in their weight-loss ambitions.

Let me tell you, I was tempted to buy that supplement because I was living what the commercial showcased. My husband and I decided to get fit together, which sounded like a great plan. We vowed to eat healthier and jog/walk three miles, four days a week. We encouraged each other, pushed each other, and celebrated our victories. As we charted our success, I soon realized that Jeff could simply think, *I would really like to lose five pounds this week,* and poof! he was down another five pounds. I, on the other hand, struggled to lose every pound. As happy as I was for my precious husband to achieve his fitness goals, I would become aggravated when he lost more weight than I did every single week.

I secretly wanted to adjust our bathroom scales' settings so he wouldn't lose more than me just one week, you know? We teased about it, but I had to really stay focused on my goals so that I wouldn't become jealous of his progress.

Whether you're jealous of your spouse's weight loss or you secretly hope your best friend, who has always been thinner than you, gets cellulite, that kind of thinking is detrimental to your journey. As my daughters often say to each other, "Don't be peanut butter and jealous!"

Sure, we joke about it, and we call jealousy cute things like "that old green-eyed monster," but in reality, jealousy is serious.

James 3:14–16 says, "But if you are bitterly jealous and there is selfish ambition in your heart, don't cover up the truth with boasting and lying. For jealousy and selfishness are not God's kind of wisdom. Such things are earthly, unspiritual, and demonic. For wherever there is jealousy and selfish ambition, there you will find disorder and evil of every kind" (NLT).

In other words, when you open up the door to jealousy, you also invite discontentment, resentment, unhappiness, anger, discouragement, strife, and so many other undesirable companions, it's very dangerous.

One of the best ways to avoid jealousy is to stay focused on your own journey and stop worrying about everyone else. Jesus doesn't want us to focus on someone else's victories or even their defeats. He doesn't want us to measure ourselves against someone else and feel like we always fall short. No, Jesus wants us to keep our eyes on the prize, to follow Him, and to allow Him to transform us for the better—spirit, mind, and body. If we waste all of our energies being jealous of someone else's accomplishments, we'll become too distracted to experience our own victories. That's why God tells us in His Word to run our own race. He knew we would be miserable trying to run somebody else's race or focusing on all the other runners.

So, no matter where you are in your wellness journey, celebrate your accomplishments along the way. If your spouse loses ten pounds in ten days, and you only lose three pounds, celebrate both of your victories. When you go shopping with your best friend and she slips on a pair of size 4 jeans and you're just now back into a size 12, don't be jealous. Instead, be thankful that you're making progress. Remember, your goal should be to become a better you, not better than somebody else. Keep your eyes on the prize. Don't waste time and energy looking at all the other runners. Instead, run your race! Your finish line is in sight—just keep pressing on!

POWER PRAYER: *Father, help me focus on my own wellness journey and not become distracted by others who are on the same path. Help me, Lord, to stay encouraged and to resist the urge to be jealous of others who might be seeing more success. In the Mighty Name of Your Son, Jesus, Amen.*

WORK YOUR WORDS: I will not be jealous or resentful when others experience success more quickly than I do. Instead, I will celebrate with them and be excited over my progress.

HEALTHY HINT: Just in case you are trying to lose weight alongside your hubby, and he is losing more quickly than you are, it's not your fault. It's a fact that men tend to have more lean muscle tissue, which of course, burns more calories than body fat, even at rest. So when men and women cut the same number of calories from their diets, men usually do lose more weight because they have more lean muscle working on their behalf. It's physiological.

CHAPTER 23

LITTLE BY LITTLE

. . . .

So, whether you eat or drink, or whatever you do,
do all to the glory of God.

1 Corinthians 10:31 (ESV)

WHEN MY GIRLS WERE LITTLE, I had to use some pretty clever maneuvering in order to get them to clean their rooms without a huge battle. So I would point to one area of their rooms and ask them to clean up that particular part. For example, Allyson used to always pile all of the clothes she had worn that day (and previous days) on top of her little rocking chair in the corner of her room, so I'd start there and say, "Ally, please hang up the clothes on your little chair." That one section didn't seem too daunting, so she rarely fought me on it. She'd happily work on that small section of the room. Then, later in the day, I'd ask her to clean out the stuff I knew she had shoved under her bed. Then, the next day we'd tackle her closet together, one section at a time, beginning with putting away the toys piled on top of her shoes.

There was a method to this madness. We accomplished

much, little by little. If I would've said to Allyson, "Clean up your entire room," she would've had an absolute fit. She would've cried and fought me every step of the way. But, one task at a time, she made progress with a good attitude because she wasn't overwhelmed.

Well, guess what? That's also a good approach to use when transforming your lifestyle into a healthier one. It's sort of that old adage, "It's a cinch by the inch but a trial by the mile" come to life. When your body is sort of like Ally's room— when many things are messed up—it's best to just tackle each area one at a time, but you don't have to go it alone. Just like I stepped in and helped Ally with her closet, God will work right alongside you and help you get you get your health in order. Isn't that good news?

As long as we make small changes on a consistent basis, we'll get there. Following are ten things we can implement, one at a time, without becoming too overwhelmed. And as we start doing these ten things on a consistent basis, our overall health will improve. Are you with me? (I wish I could give you a "fist bump" or a "high five" through the pages of this book.)

- Use sea salt instead of table salt.
- Replace bleached flour with unbleached flour.
- Add cayenne pepper to your diet every day. (Yes, it's a little hot but very yummy, and it's been known to speed up your metabolism.)

- Replace soda and sugary juices with water. (To make water more palatable, add lemon or lime slices and some natural stevia to sweeten to your liking.)
- Add more fiber to your daily diet.
- Opt for applesauce instead of oil when a recipe calls for oil.
- Eat five fruits and vegetables every day.
- Try baking, broiling, or grilling food instead of frying.
- When going out to eat, drink several glasses of water prior to arriving so that you aren't ravenous before ordering. (Also, if you have a bread addiction, take only one piece and ask the server to remove the bread basket from the table. If it's not on the table, you can't eat it.)
- When you really want a muffin or a cookie, choose a protein bar instead. (There are many yummy varieties. Not sure which one to choose? Here's a great article that highlights the best ones on the market: http://www.bodybuilding.com/store/best-protein-bars.html.)

All right, we can do this! With God, we can do all things. And, hey, if you mess up and eat some french fries, it's okay. This isn't an all-or-nothing kind of thing, remember? It's about progress, not perfection. Be excited! We're getting healthy together!

POWER PRAYER: *Father, thank You for loving me and going on this health journey with me. Help me, Lord, to implement these tips for healthy eating and make them a part of my lifestyle. I know I can do all things with You on my side. In the Mighty Name of Your Son, Jesus. Amen.*

WORK YOUR WORDS: I choose to do better every day in the areas of my eating and working out. I choose to be healthy.

HEALTHY HINT: Here's another health tip regarding going out to eat. If you know which restaurant you're going to ahead of time, go online and look at their menu. That way, you won't feel the pressure of "on the spot" ordering. You'll have time to look at the restaurant's healthy options and know before you arrive what you're going to order.

CHAPTER 24

MAKE THE MOST OF YOUR TIME

. . . .

*Look carefully then how you walk, not as unwise
but as wise, making the best use of the time,
because the days are evil. Therefore do not be foolish,
but understand what the will of the Lord is.*

Ephesians 5:15–17 (ESV)

OSCAR WILDE ONCE SAID, "No man is rich enough to buy back his past." In other words, time is our most valuable asset. We can't get back the minutes we spend on menial things, so let's decide to use our minutes wisely.

If you think of time as your most valuable asset, you'll start investing in more important things and limit the time you spend on the not-so-important stuff. Can you recognize the time-stealers in your life? Television is probably the most universal time-stealer: One reality TV show leads to another or one ball game leads to another. Before you know it, the entire night is gone. Our cell phones are another great time-stealer. Whether you are Instagram crazy or texting everyone in your contact list or actually talking on the phone with a super gabby friend (you know the one!), many minutes can be eaten up on your cell. And what about Facebook? You promise yourself you'll quickly read through your newsfeed, and two hours later you have stalked, commented, and liked until your fingers are sore from typing. Not that any of these time-stealing activities are necessarily bad, but if they are keeping you from doing something God wants you to do, then they are hindering your obedience. Get on board with God's plan.

Let's make time for fitness and eating healthy.

Let's be honest: Working out and preparing healthy food can be time-consuming, but those minutes you invest will be more than worth it. I know it's easier and quicker to drive through a fast food restaurant (and that's okay once in a while because most fast food franchises have a few healthy options), but with a little planning and some storage containers, you can make good use of your time. Many experts suggest prepping your meals ahead of time, maybe on the weekend, when you have more time for preparation. Need some healthy meal ideas? There are several great websites that offer free recipes and downloadable cookbooks with ingredients, instructions, and nutritional information provided.

As for making time for fitness, you just have to find it. Remember that you don't have to devote two hours in the gym every day to see results. In fact, you don't even have to do your workout all at once if your schedule doesn't allow for an uninterrupted thirty minutes. Try ten minutes in the morning, ten minutes during your lunch break, and ten minutes after dinner. If you need help knowing what to do during those ten minutes, there are several apps you might enjoy. My favorite is called the "7minuteworkoutchallenge" and I love it! It offers twelve high-intensity bodyweight exercises, thirty seconds per exercise, with ten seconds of rest between exercises, and at the end of that seven-minute challenge, you know you've made the most of those minutes. Also, it is voice-prompted so you don't have to worry with a timer. If that is not the one for you, keep looking until you find one you like.

Just by making up your mind that you will use your time more wisely, you'll be surprised how much more you'll be able to get done in a twenty-four-hour period. Remember to ask God to help you carve out time for your health. He will!

POWER PRAYER: *Father, thank You for helping me prioritize my days so that I can find time to prepare healthy meals and work in workouts. I commit this day to You. In the Mighty Name of Your Son, Jesus, Amen.*

WORK YOUR WORDS: I will use my time wisely. I will find time for preparing healthy meals and find time to work out.

HEALTHY HINT: Let's be real—rarely do I wake up and want to work out. So I find that if I do certain things, I am more motivated to exercise. For example, since I work from home, I put on my workout clothes when I first get up so that I am already dressed for success. If I'm dressed to work out, I usually do. I bet this trick will work for you, too.

CHAPTER 25

GET SWEATY TOGETHER

. . . .

*Most important of all, continue to show deep love
for each other, for love covers a multitude of sins.*

1 Peter 4:8 (NLT)

EVER HEARD THE EXPRESSION, "Couples who sweat together, stay together"? Well, it's a common mantra in the workout world, and it's actually a fact. I recently read an article called "The Perfect Workout Partner," and I was truly intrigued by what Dr. Jane Greer, a marriage and relationship psychotherapist, had to say.

"When a couple works out together, the actual exercise itself can physically and emotionally have a positive impact," she said. "Both partners come away with feelings of synchronicity, cooperative spirit and shared passion. Then you throw in some spicy endorphins and it can be a real power trip for the relationship."

It's almost like "date night" at the gym, and any "us" time is precious in today's busy life, right? I remember those seasons of craziness. You know, when you find yourself in bleachers somewhere every night, watching your kiddos play whatever sport they're playing that night, and then there's the church and social commitments, too. Add all of that to your already busy work schedule, and it's a miracle to find time for fitness or any quality time with your significant other. So, why not kill two birds with one stone, so to speak. Work out with that special someone!

Need some ideas? Here are a few that my hubby, Jeff, and I enjoy:

- **Take a hike together.** Whether you're hiking a trail at a leisurely pace, holding hands, and chatting about the day's events, or hoofing it up a mountain with little talking and lots of huffing and puffing, getting outdoors together is special.

- **Turn your power walk into a walk of love.** Okay, so maybe you're both power-walking or even jogging so talking or holding hands isn't an option, but after you've pushed yourself to your limit, use the cool-down time to walk side by side and converse in your Converse. (See what I did there?)

- **Strength train to strengthen your bond.** You need someone to spot you when you're lifting weights anyway, right? So who better than your best friend, your significant other, your babe? Jeff and I did the Body for Life program together several years ago, and it was amazing how much harder I pushed myself when he was at the gym with me. We encouraged each other and celebrated each other's progress. Plus, let's be honest, seeing your man looking sweaty and "muscley" in his tank top is kind of hot . . . and I don't just mean temperature-wise. ;)

- **Make hug stops.** So you know you're supposed to shoot for 10,000 steps a day, right? Well, even if your significant other can't go with you to the gym or hit the trail, you can still include him while getting in your steps. For example, let's say he can't go with you to the gym tonight because he has to do some work in his office. Of course you understand, but as you're doing your own work or whatever your evening plans are, stop by his home office/study and simply give him a hug and a kiss. An hour later, step into his office and see if he needs anything. You might say, "Coffee? Tea? Me?" haha. And then give him another hug. You've accomplished two things in this scenario. You've added more steps to your daily count by walking around the house every hour, and you've made your husband feel loved and appreciated by your little bursts of affection. It's a win/win!

So, get your workout on together! It only makes sense to work on your overall health with the person you love most in the world. You can cheer each other on to a healthier, fit body and celebrate many more years together. Jeff and I are at twenty-four years and counting, and it just keeps getting better and better . . . yay!

POWER PRAYER: *Father, thank You for the special people You have placed in my life. I am so grateful for (insert the name of your guy), and I am asking You to help me love him like You love him. Also, Lord, help us to find more quality time together, whether that be in the gym or fishing or grabbing a Starbucks together. I love You, Lord. In the Mighty Name of Your Son, Jesus, Amen.*

WORK YOUR WORDS: I choose to love every day and to work on my relationships.

HEALTHY HINT: When you're training with your guy, it's also much easier to eat healthy because you're eating the same stuff. In other words, you don't have to fix Paleo for you and mac 'n cheese and corn dogs for him. Also, when you do enjoy cheat days on your eating program, you can "cheat" together. You can dine at your favorite restaurant and share each other's desserts without any guilt, just pure joy . . . because you know you're going to hit it hard in the gym the next day.

CHAPTER 26

HERE COMES
THE JUDGE

. . . .

*"By this all men will know that you are
my disciples, if you love one another."*
John 13:35 (NIV)

I TRAVEL QUITE A BIT teaching at women's conferences and writers' events, and I love to go to church in
whatever city I happen to be in on that particular Sunday.
From Catholic to Methodist to Assembly of God—I've
attended church services in pretty much every denomination
and have been blessed by the message and the people. But
there was one Sunday when I wished I'd stayed in my hotel
room and watched a TV minister instead.

We had just finished the praise and worship portion of
the service when the pastor's wife came up to the podium.
I assumed she was there to welcome the congregation, but I
couldn't have been more wrong. She proceeded to take ten
minutes scold those who were not dressed to her liking, stating

that people should dress up when they come to church out of reverence to God.

As she continued her rant, I felt so ashamed. Not because I wasn't dressed appropriately by her standards—because I was—but rather because she was misrepresenting my Heavenly Father. I wondered if she had considered that the old blue jeans and holey T-shirt might have been that person's *only* outfit. I wondered if she realized that not every person in the auditorium had enough money for food, let alone a new wardrobe. I wondered how someone with so much biblical knowledge could behave so badly.

And I wondered if I'd ever been guilty of that same judgmental attitude. I hoped I hadn't, but I asked God that very morning to help me see people through His eyes, not my own. I was pretty sure I'd never judged folks for their attire, but I was still convicted because I knew I had been judgmental in other ways. I was no better than this "judge-y pastor's wife" if I was being honest with myself and God.

You see, I have always been in the battle of the bulge—staying fit is a daily fight for me. I've never been able to go up to an all-you-can-eat buffet and actually eat all that I wanted. So, whenever I'd see someone else going up and heaping mounds of food onto plate after plate, I am sorry to say I judged that person. If that woman with the healthy appetite was smaller than I happened to be at that time, I'd think, *Well, she'd better enjoy it while she can, because when her metabolism slows down, she won't be able to eat like that.* Or if the woman was larger than me, I'd think: *No wonder she is so heavy. She eats way too much. . . .*

Those judgments were ugly and probably not even accurate. Maybe the younger, thinner gal could only afford one meal that day so she was making the most of it, getting all the "bang for her buck," so to speak. And maybe the larger woman came up with a clean plate to get more food several times because she was serving her husband, who wasn't able to get up and get his own food. Who knows? And more importantly, who cares? It wasn't my place to judge.

I feel convicted confessing my previous judgmental attitude even now—years later—but thank God, He did a work in my heart. And if you find yourself in that judgmental state of mind, He can do a work in your heart too.

Next time you're tempted to judge someone, stop yourself and pray for that person instead. You can't pray for someone and judge that person at the same time. Bottom line, you don't know that person's story. And, hey, while you're at it, quit being so hard on yourself. If you're in that "self-loathing mode," it's time to stop being so harsh and judgmental when it comes to you. Don't let the devil talk you into hating yourself so much that you don't even feel worthy of taking care of yourself or hoping for a better, healthier, happier life. You are a child of the Most High God!

As Christians, we aren't called to judge; we're called to love—that goes for loving others and yourself.

We used to sing a powerful chorus at Camp Wildwood

Church Camp that said, "They'll know we are Christians by our love, by our love, yes, they'll know we are Christians by our love." There's a lot of truth in that little song. Let's start living those lyrics on a daily basis.

POWER PRAYER: *Father, help me to see people through Your eyes, and help me to lose the judgmental attitude. In the Mighty Name of Your Son, Jesus, Amen.*

WORK YOUR WORDS: I will not judge others; instead I will pray for them.

HEALTHY HINT: All-you-can-eat buffets can be problematic when you're trying to lose weight, so you have to be strategic and fill up on the healthy stuff first. Make sure you begin with salad, fruits, and veggies. And just because you're allowed unlimited refills on that soda doesn't mean you should. Opt for water with lemon instead. Lastly, remember that your brain and your stomach don't register feelings of "being full" at the point of being satisfied . . . it can take up to thirty minutes, so chew slowly to avoid eating past the point of being full.

CHAPTER 27

CONFIDENCE IS ATTRACTIVE

. . . .

Therefore, as God's chosen people, holy and dearly loved,
clothe yourselves with compassion, kindness,
humility, gentleness and patience.

Colossians 3:12 (NIV)

WHILE RESEARCHING for a book assignment several years ago, I spent many hours studying the life of Eleanor Roosevelt. Sure, I knew a bit about her from a US history class in high school, but I had no idea just how amazing she was or how much her words would impact me.

It's no wonder why Eleanor Roosevelt has been called the most revered woman of her generation. She made a difference every place she ever dwelled. She not only gave birth to six children, but she also served as a dynamic political helpmate to her husband, Franklin Delano Roosevelt.

Eleanor Roosevelt literally transformed the role of First Lady, holding press conferences, traveling to all parts of the country, giving lectures and radio broadcasts, and expressing her opinions in a daily syndicated newspaper column called "My Day." You might say she was a spitfire, a woman on a mission, a servant to mankind, a loving wife and mother, and a role model for all women.

Knowing of her accomplishments, it was very interesting to discover that Mrs. Roosevelt was a very shy, very plain, and very awkward child. It wasn't until she began attending a distinguished school in England that she developed self-confidence, realizing that her inner beauty and fortitude would make a way for her. During that self-discovery phase, she wrote these words of wisdom: "No matter how plain a woman may be if truth and loyalty are stamped upon her face, all will be attracted to her."

Wow.

If only we all understood that truth and could actually believe it.

For years, society has told us that if we're not beautiful—like the cover girls on magazines—then we will not be successful, and we'll never truly have a place in this world. Many women feel they don't fit in simply because they don't fit into a size 6 suit. Maybe you feel that way.

Too many wonderful women have bought the lie, and some are still buying that lie. In fact, just recently I noticed a new trend on Facebook called the "Beautiful Woman Challenge," where someone challenges a friend to post five pictures that make her *feel* beautiful. Seems like an easy task, yet I've read comments from some who refuse to accept the challenge, such as one that absolutely broke my heart. The woman wrote: "Sorry, I will not be participating in this challenge because I don't feel beautiful in any photo." Instead of posting a picture of herself on her wedding day, or when she was pregnant with her daughter, or at a family reunion surrounded by all of her loved ones, she chose to boycott the challenge because of a "lack of beauty." I so wanted to reach out to her and say, "You are beautiful. You are exactly who God created you to be. You are a wonderful wife and mother. You make a difference in your corner of the world."

Ladies, it's time we realize our worth, knowing that it's not determined by a number on the bathroom scales or the number of "likes" we receive on our new profile picture. It's time we focus on our assets and not our flaws. And, like Eleanor Roosevelt, it's time we celebrate who we are, overcome our lack of confidence, and change our world.

It's not what's on the outside that makes us worthy, lovely, and attractive. That kind of beauty is fleeting. It's loyalty, truth, and love on the inside that draws people to us. In other words, it's the Jesus in us that makes us irresistible. And when we finally get to a place where we believe that we matter, that we're valuable, that we're beautiful in our own way, then we will be able to fulfill our divine destinies.

So if you are feeling plain, unworthy, unattractive, or unnoticed—give yourself a makeover from the inside out. Ask God, the Master Makeover Artist, to develop the fruit of the Spirit within you, so that you might become so lovely on the inside that it spills out onto everyone you encounter. Pretty soon, you'll be confident and irresistible. And, like Eleanor Roosevelt, you'll make a difference every place you go!

POWER PRAYER: *Father, help me to realize my worth isn't measured by a size of clothing or the number on my bathroom scales. Help me, Lord, to develop more self-confidence so that I can better fulfill my destiny in You. Give me a makeover, Lord, from the inside out. In the Mighty Name of Your Son, Jesus, Amen.*

WORK YOUR WORDS: I am strong, confident, and mighty in the Lord, and His love, which is bubbling up inside my heart, makes me simply irresistible.

HEALTHY HINT: If you become easily discouraged on your journey to becoming a leaner, healthier version of yourself, resist weighing yourself daily. Experts agree that weighing yourself once a week or even once every other week is a much better plan. Neither your self-worth nor your level of joy should be determined by your digital scales.

STRENGTH
TRAINING

. . . .

CHAPTER 28

GET A FRESH START

. . . .

Don't brashly announce what you're going to do tomorrow;
you don't know the first thing about tomorrow.

Proverbs 27:1 (MSG)

I COME FROM A LONG LINE of perpetual dieters. I probably heard my mama say, "I'm starting my diet on Monday" at least a hundred times growing up. And, unfortunately, I have carried on this family tradition. Over the years, I've made many "Monday morning resolutions." Know what I mean? I get up on Monday with great ambition and determination, ready to begin that latest, greatest diet. With my approved food list in hand, I head for the supermarket to purchase everything I need to succeed. Feeling confident and excited, I power through my day, all the while sipping lemon water and thinking about the next approved meal. I call all my friends and talk to them about my new diet and try to convince one or two of them to go on it with me. I surf the Internet, reading all of the success stories surrounding my new diet, and get even more pumped about my decision to do this plan. I head outside for a power walk, lemon water in hand, and accomplish the daily recommended cardio. And after returning, I realize I've already consumed all of my approved foods for the day. I resist temptation as my husband eats a grilled cheese and bacon sandwich right in front of me, and head upstairs to shower. I've almost made it an entire day on my new diet, but as the night continues, my hunger grows. By 9 p.m., I've already cheated . . . twice.

Okay, some weeks I actually make it to Wednesday or Thursday before cheating (depending on how strict the new diet is), which is why I make the old go-to declaration: "I'm starting my diet on Monday."

Sound familiar?

Are you also a chronic dieter? Always starting your diet on Monday?

Well, at least we feel each other's pain. And I've got good news. Your "I'm starting my new diet on Monday" phase of life is now over. We are moving forward with wisdom, excitement, and confidence, knowing that Almighty God is leading the way. We can do this, and here's how. We learn from our mistakes.

Mistake #1: Diets never work, and here's why: Because the very concept of going on a diet means you have to eventually go off of it. That means it's not a way of life, meaning that when you go off of that diet, you most likely will return to the old bad habits that caused you to need a diet in the first place. So, say this with me, "Diets are stupid." (That felt good, didn't it?)

Mistake #2: The all-or-nothing mentality is also stupid. So what if you mess up on your new healthy eating plan? It's not the end of the world. Don't punish yourself, vowing to start again on Monday. Don't wait to get back on the horse; just start again right at that moment! Remember, we're striving for progress, not perfection.

Mistake #3: We try to go it alone. Why do we try to adopt a healthy lifestyle and make life-altering changes without involving our Heavenly Father? He is the missing piece that makes this whole thing work. With God all things are possible!

So this is the day when we make a fresh start. Don't wait until Monday (unless today is actually Monday). No more crazy diets that you'll have to cheat on by noon. Instead, we will simply do the "do's" and implement healthy eating little by little. And if we mess up and have two pieces of cake at the office party, don't worry about it. Just begin again. Don't punish yourself or feel guilty or give up. Instead, just move forward and ask God to help you.

POWER PRAYER: *Father, thank You for getting involved in my healthy eating. And thank You, Lord, for helping me make these healthy changes and break the family tradition of always starting a new diet on Monday. I love You, Lord. In the Mighty Name of Your Son, Jesus, Amen.*

WORK YOUR WORDS: I will begin healthy eating today! This very day I break that awful cycle of always starting a new diet on Monday.

HEALTHY HINT: One tip that can help you stay on track with healthy eating is to simply record what you're eating, following the rule: "If you bite it, you write it." By keeping a food diary, you can chart your progress and learn from your patterns. In fact, recent studies reveal that people who kept a food diary six days a week lost about twice as much weight as those who only kept records one day a week or less.

CHAPTER 29

VERY TEMPTING . . .

. . . .

God is faithful; he will not let you be tempted beyond
what you can bear. But when you are tempted, he will also
provide a way out so that you can stand up under it.

1 Corinthians 10:13 (NIV)

SO, YOU'VE BEEN ON THE GO all day, and before you know it, it's almost 5 p.m. No wonder you're hungry! It's been hours since you've had any food. Your stomach is growling. You're a little light-headed. And you're becoming more perturbed by the minute. That's what we call "hangry." When this happens, you need food, and you need it pronto. So it's always a good idea to carry a baggie of almonds or a banana or a protein bar in your purse for times such as this, because if you don't . . . temptation will more than likely get the best of you.

Trust me, I speak from experience.

When I don't have a healthy alternative with me, I reach for a Snickers at the checkout line, or I drive through a fast food restaurant for a greasy burger, or a chocolate milk shake from my favorite ice cream place. All of those yummy options are hard enough to resist when I'm not hungry but when I'm overly hungry, I almost can't say no.

We are faced with temptations on a daily basis—some physical and some spiritual. And our flesh can be quite persuasive, wanting its own way. Whether it be a temptation to tell a little white lie, to overeat, to be lazy, or to tell off the woman who stole your parking spot at Walmart, temptations are real. Every single day we have to choose to resist those temptations and follow God. Some days, it's a real struggle.

Aren't you thankful that we always have God on our side, giving us strength and courage to ward off even the most tempting of temptations? Galatians 5:22–23 tells us, "But the Holy Spirit produces this kind of fruit in our lives: love, joy, peace, patience, kindness, goodness, faithfulness, gentleness, and self-control" (NLT).

These wonderful attributes are better known as the fruit of the Spirit, and as Christians, those "fruit" should be operating in our lives. The last one mentioned, "self-control," is a must as we battle our fleshly nature and say no to those temptations. So pray Galatians 5:22-23 over yourself every morning, saying: "Thank You, Lord, that I have an abundance of love, joy, peace, patience, kindness, goodness, faithfulness, gentleness, and self-control within me. Amen."

While much of this is a spiritual battle, there are some practical things we can do to ward off temptation and make it easier to walk away, such as:

Get enough sleep: The studies are pretty clear when it comes to sleep and hunger. Research shows that sleep deprivation leads to increases in ghrelin (a hormone that signals to your brain that you're hungry), which leads to overeating. See, there's a reason we crave carbs and overeat when we're tired, so get enough sleep at night.

Know when we're hungry versus being emotionally taxed: When we become emotional, upset, or fearful, we often reach for comfort foods like sugary treats, pizza, or buttery mashed potatoes. Initially we feel better, because these types of foods actually spike certain neurotransmitters in the brain that cause an elevated feeling. But the crash always comes later, so don't give in to those temptations. Instead, take a moment to worship God. Sing. Pray. Or meditate on a few scriptures such as "I can do all things through Christ who strengthens me" (Philippians 4:13, NKJV).

Hydrate: Mild dehydration can easily be mistaken for hunger, so we often eat when we really should down a bottle of water. Knowing this, it's important to drink plenty of water throughout the day so that you don't become dehydrated and overeat. And experts agree that it's a good idea to drink a glass of water about twenty minutes before a meal, curbing your appetite and filling you up enough so that you don't give in to that package of crumb cakes in the office vending machine.

Although being tempted is a reality of life on this earth, we are overcomers through Christ Jesus, and we already possess all of the self-control we'll ever need. Be encouraged! Temptations do not have control over you anymore. It's the other way around—whoo-hoo!

POWER PRAYER: *Father, help me resist temptation in every area of my life. Through You, I know I am an overcomer and can practice self-control and discipline. Thank You, Lord, for reworking me from the inside out so that I am more like You. In the Mighty Name of Your Son, Jesus, Amen.*

WORK YOUR WORDS: I will make healthy choices all throughout my day. I can and will resist temptations because I can do all things through Christ Jesus!

HEALTHY HINT: When it comes to food temptation, the best way to resist is simple. Don't keep them in the house. So if powdered white doughnuts are your weakness, then don't buy them on your next grocery trip. If they are out of sight, they'll more likely be out of mind.

CHAPTER 30

SPOT-ON

. . . .

Therefore if anyone is in Christ, he is a new creature;
the old things passed away; behold, new things have come."
2 Corinthians 5:17 (NASB)

OVER THE COURSE OF MY LIFE, I've been certified through Mary Mayta's Fit For Life Certification, the Aerobics and Fitness Association of America, Zumba International Network, and American Sports and Fitness.

Since graduating from high school, I have taught at Fit For Life, the Indiana University (IU) Fit staff, the Bloomington (IN) YMCA, Rick's Gym, and Priority Fitness. I even ran my own lunchtime fitness business, "Body Basics," in the mid-nineties while working full-time as a reporter for my local newspaper. And now I lead a class at Priority Fitness called "Fitness 101." I have also served as the health and fitness writer for a LifeWay magazine, as well as ghostwritten several fitness books. In other words, I have been involved in the world of fitness in one way or another since I was eighteen years old, and even before then, I was working out with Jane Fonda.

Remember the old exercise VHS tapes when Jane Fonda would make you do a million buttocks lifts, and then say, "Now, go for the burn!"? Yeah, me too. Then I progressed to *Buns of Steel, Abs of Steel,* and *Legs of Steel,* though none of my body parts ever looked like steel. And how could any of us forget the "Thighmaster" contraption? (It's currently under my bed, along with a few friendly dust bunnies.)

But in all of those years, I never saw "spot reducing" actually produce the results that were promised. Bottom line, spot reducing doesn't work all by itself because if you tighten and tone the muscles in your backside, but there is still a whole lot of fat on top of that muscle, you're not going to see the results you desire. Sadly, you won't have that Brazilian bum you were promised if you're carrying a lot of extra weight on top of your toned glutes. That's why spot reducing alone never produces the results you're desiring if you don't also participate in some sort of cardio activity three to four times a week to burn away the fat. (And, of course, diet is a critical factor in achieving the desired results, as well.)

I've got news for you: Spot reducing in the spiritual realm doesn't work that well, either. If you just work on your anger problem, but you leave those six inches of unforgiveness untouched, it won't really make a difference. Or, if you work hard memorizing scriptures in order to build your faith, but you still have a layer of sin covering your heart, it's just a memorization activity.

Here's the good news: In the spiritual realm, you don't

have to do intense cardio workouts to get rid of those layers of sin. It's much easier. All you have to do is confess your sins and ask God to forgive you. The Word says He will! Then He will help you "spot reduce" until your spiritual life is as fit as Fonda in her leg-warmer-wearing, prime-fitness years. You don't have to go for the burn. You just have to go to God!

POWER PRAYER: *Father, I want to live a happy, whole, fulfilling life, and I know I cannot do that apart from You. So, I repent of my sins right now and ask You to forgive me so that I can go forward and fulfill my destiny in You. I give You all of the anger, unforgiveness, and bitterness that have been plaguing my heart and life, and I thank You for replacing them with Your love, joy, and peace. Thank You for seeing the best in me and helping me become spiritually fit to do the work in the kingdom that needs to be done, and thank You for helping me as I become physically fit, as well. In the Mighty Name of Your Son, Jesus, Amen.*

WORK YOUR WORDS: I will not participate in spot reduction in the physical or spiritual realms. I will allow God to shape me spiritually, and I will combine cardio and strength training to produce the desired results in the physical realm.

HEALTHY HINT: A combination of strength training and cardio is your best bet when trying to torch fat, because study after study has proven that a plethora of exercises for a particular area does not produce weight loss in that one area. Thus, spot reducing doesn't work—ever.

CHAPTER 31

HANG ON TO YOUR HOPE

. . . .

Jesus looked at them and said, "With man this is impossible,
but with God all things are possible."

Matthew 19:26 (NIV)

I RECENTLY HAD A FRIEND go through some health issues, and the medicine they put her on caused her to gain a substantial amount of weight. She had always been a very small person, but with the forty extra pounds on her small frame, she looked and felt very different. She was so distraught over the weight gain, I could hear it in her voice when she called me.

"I need prayer. I need help. I need hope."

Life had dealt her some doozies, and as she put it, she was simply "done." This extra weight was the final straw, and it had taken its toll on her self-esteem. She admitted that she was hardly leaving the house because she was so distraught.

She almost couldn't receive what I had to say because her

hurt ran so deep. She hadn't lost her faith in God, but she had lost her joy, and she had definitely lost her hope.

Hopelessness.

If you've ever experienced it, you know how awful it feels. Hopelessness sucks you dry of any joy, peace, or victory in your life. In fact, hopelessness can be almost suffocating, stealing the Word from your heart and blanketing you with heaviness. When hopelessness sets up camp in your heart, it leaves no room for happiness. Bottom line—hopelessness is not of God.

Actually, Satan is the king of hopelessness. He loves to get out his big old magnifying glass and have you look through it. He'll show you all of the problems in your life and whisper, "Look how big they are! Your problems are beyond fixing. They are too big for God." But let me tell you something: Satan is also the father of all lies. So if he tells you that your problems are too big for God, you can boldly say, "Liar, liar, pants on fire! Nothing is impossible for my God!"

You may have lost your hope today; well, I have such good news for you. We can get your hope back right now. You say, "But Michelle, you can't fix my problem." You're right, I can't. But I'll tell you what I told my friend: I know Someone who can—our Heavenly Father. Not only can He fix your problems, He is willing to do so. But you have to do your part. You have to get your faith on. You have to believe that He is able to do all things, and then stand on that promise. You have to believe that God will come through for you—no matter how bad the circumstances appear.

So when the devil whispers in your ear, "You'll never lose this weight. You'll never be fit again," you can boldly say: "I can do all things through Christ who strengthens me! And you're a liar, Satan!" And when the scales aren't moving in the right direction though you're trying desperately to lose weight, you have to know that God is on this journey with you, and that He promises to never leave you.

Do you believe?

Be encouraged today! Begin praising God for your breakthrough and keep that heart of gratitude in spite of the circumstances. Hang on to your hope! There is no circumstance, no problem, no amount of weight, no health crisis—nothing—that is too big for our God!

POWER PRAYER: *Lord, I am feeling hopeless today. I am overwhelmed with the problems in my life, but I know that You are able to do all things. And I am asking You to intervene on my behalf. I praise You today for the victories that are yet to come. Please remove the hopelessness from my heart and replace it with supernatural happiness. Let my life bring glory and honor to You and encourage those around me. Thank You, God, for never leaving me. In the Mighty Name of Your Son, Jesus, Amen.*

WORK YOUR WORDS: I am hopeful because I know that God is with me and that His Word is true. I also know that Satan is a liar!

HEALTHY HINT: If you've been working out, putting in the cardio and strength training, yet your weight is staying about the same—don't give up! Don't lose hope! Here's the truth: You're simply building muscle, and muscle has a much greater density than fat. That means it takes up less volume than an equal amount of fat. So you could actually look slimmer without a big drop (or any drop) in weight.

CHAPTER 32

GOT WATER?

. . . .

"Whoever believes in me, as the Scripture has said,
streams of living water will flow from within him."
John 7:38 (NIV)

AGUA. H_2O. WATER. You can call it whatever you want as long as you drink lots of it. I learned about the power of water while on vacation with my niece Autumn several years ago.

Spring break was quickly approaching, and our entire family began doubling up on cardio workouts and cutting back on calories, in hopes of shedding a few more pounds and inches before we donned our bathing suits on the beach. Autumn and I had been doing the same eating program all spring and had both seen great results. But I had sort of plateaued, and she continued to lose at a steady pace. So, when we were all staying in the same condominium that week in Florida, I studied her eating habits. I was in search of her secret—what was she doing to continue losing weight while my weight loss had halted? What was the missing puzzle piece? After a few days of stalking her, I had my answer.

While I consumed a few bottles of water daily, I also downed several bottles of diet soda, topped off with a touch of regular soda to kill that awful aftertaste, while Autumn drank only water. I asked her about it, and she confessed she had given up all soda—diet and regular—several weeks earlier. The more research I did about diet soda, the more I discovered how smart Autumn had been to give up that vice.

Research shows that diet soda can actually trigger something in you that makes you crave sugar. Also, a 2005 study found a 41 percent increase in obesity risk associated with each serving of diet soda consumed daily. When I read that, I almost passed out! There's more, too. A study featured in the March issue of the *Journal of the American Geriatrics Society* found that people who drank diet soda gained almost triple the abdominal fat over nine years as those who didn't drink diet soda. Yikes!

Let me tell you, kicking the soda habit isn't easy. I've quit for months at a time, gone "cold turkey," and lived to tell about it. But the minute I allowed myself even one Polar Pop filled with Coke Zero and a squirt of cherry, I was hooked all over again. (I've repeated this cycle several times over the past few years. You'd think I'd learn—ugh!)

Seriously, kicking the soda habit and drinking mainly water is one of the best decisions you can make for your overall health. Not only does water suppress the appetite naturally, but also it helps the body metabolize stored fat.

Here are some additional water facts to get you motivated to drink at least 64 ounces of water each day:

- Water maintains blood volume and proper muscle tone.
- Water can improve the appearance of your skin.
- Water is a great treatment for fluid retention.
- Water keeps you from being dehydrated. (Did you know that one of the most common reasons for headaches and anxiety attacks is dehydration?)

Okay, now that you're convinced you should be drinking H_2O, I want to talk about another kind of water—the Living Water. If you've asked Jesus to be the Lord of your life, you're filled with the Holy Spirit, which is the Living Water. This water will make you beautiful on the inside and spiritually fit.

The Word talks of the Living Water in John chapter 4. Remember the Samaritan woman whom Jesus met at the well? She was shocked when Jesus asked her for a drink of water, because He was a Jew. He spoke to her, saying, "Everyone who drinks this water will be thirsty again, but whoever drinks the water I give him will never thirst. Indeed, the water I give him will become in him a spring of water welling up to eternal life" (verses 13 and 14, NIV).

Let that Living Water (the Holy Spirit) stir on the inside of you today, and let it spill out onto all you encounter. You just never know when a "Samaritan woman" might be watching and wondering what makes you different. When she asks for a "drink," you'll be able to offer her the Living Water that you've been given. That's one secret you'll want to share!

POWER PRAYER: *Father, help me to crave water so that I will drink at least 64 ounces every day, and Lord, fill me with Your Living Water that I might be a witness to all whom I encounter. In the Mighty Name of Your Son, Jesus, Amen.*

WORK YOUR WORDS: I will be deliberate about drinking more water—both physically and spiritually.

HEALTHY HINT: It's good to spread out your water consumption throughout the day. Need help remembering to drink up? Try one of the new motivational water bottles that are timed for you, marking off how many ounces you should drink by a certain time. They are so helpful and usually have motivational writing on them for an added bonus.

CHAPTER 33

GRACE FOR TODAY

· ·

"Don't worry about tomorrow. It will take care of itself.
You have enough to worry about today."
Matthew 6:34 (CEV)

TRYING TO GET FIT or lose weight or both can be over-whelming at times. Trust me; I get it. Earlier this year, I had to have my gallbladder removed. Of course, this caused me to change my entire diet, because without a gallbladder, your body can't process some of the foods it's always processed quite as well. Anyway, this presented a big problem for me, and the worst part was, I knew it wasn't just a fad diet that I could follow for a few days, drop seven pounds, and then go back to my normal eating. This health issue had forced me to change my entire way of eating and find a "new normal," and I wasn't happy about it.

In fact, I was quite grumpy about the whole thing.

Before I had the surgery, I read many articles about it. And I talked to lots of people who had already gone through this common procedure. From what I'd learned, recovery time seemed to be fairly short, so I tried to stay positive. In fact, some patients reported having their gallbladder removed on Friday and going back to work on the following Monday, so I was sure I'd be in that group. After all, I was pretty physically fit going into the surgery with no other health complications. I was optimistic. I was sure I'd be walking a mile the day after surgery.

I was wrong.

I not only couldn't walk a mile the next day, I couldn't even climb in and out of bed by myself. I was so sore—even my hair hurt. I wasn't able to walk a mile without hurting for ten days. (I knew at that point, I was starting at ground zero with my workouts.) The recovery was much slower than I'd anticipated, and even though I was eating the cleanest and healthiest I'd eaten in my whole life, my weight stagnated. The only way the scales seemed to move were up!

How is this possible?! I wondered.

At my follow-up appointment, I expressed my concerns to my doctor, who assured me that what I was experiencing was very normal and that my body would figure out how to operate without a gallbladder soon enough. He assured me that my weight would stabilize and that I'd be able to work out hard again before much longer.

Meanwhile, he encouraged me to continue with my healthy eating and watch my fat and carb intake.

What does he want me to eat, air?! I questioned in my head.

It was during this season that I learned a very important

spiritual lesson—God gives us the grace that we need every single day. As I was retraining myself to eat more vegetables and less processed food, the struggle was real. I couldn't think too far ahead about missing out on all the yummy fried and chocolate-covered foods I'd always loved in moderation. Instead, I had to focus on God and trust Him to retrain my taste buds.

And, yes, I had a few breakdowns along the way, but I learned that I didn't have to worry about eating healthy and increasing my core work the following day or the next week. I only had to trust God for the grace to get through that day.

That seemed way more doable.

And that's how I've found success—not only when dealing with my physical body, but also in my spiritual walk. God gives us enough grace for today. You can't store it up for tomorrow, but you can trust Him that He will have grace readily available for you the moment you need it.

Just trust Him.

POWER PRAYER: *Father, thank You for giving me exactly enough grace for today. You are more than enough! Help me, Lord, to trust You more, not only on this journey to become healthy, but in every area of my life. I love You, and I'm thankful for Your love and faithfulness. In the Mighty Name of Your Son, Jesus, Amen.*

WORK YOUR WORDS: I am going to keep my eyes fixed on You, Lord, and do what I have to do today. I am not worried about tomorrow because I know You have grace for me then and forevermore.

HEALTHY HINT: Sometimes just seeing your progress will give you that extra motivation to make it another day. So, if you have a goal of losing fifty pounds, for example, get two glass jars. In one, put fifty pretty marbles and write on the front "Pounds to Lose." And write "Pounds Lost" on the other. As you lose a pound, transfer one marble from the "Pounds to Lose" jar to the "Pounds Lost" jar. Seeing that marble transfer is a visual reminder you're doing great!

CHAPTER 34

KEEP ON KEEPING ON!

. . . .

I don't mean to say that I have already achieved
these things or that I have already reached perfection.
But I press on to possess that perfection for which
Christ Jesus first possessed me.

Philippians 3:12 (NLT)

WHEN I LOOK AT PEOPLE who train at the gym where I go, I am often in awe of them. Currently, there's a woman in her sixties who is usually on the treadmill next to me, and she has the body of someone much younger. In fact, I'm pretty sure she could kick my hiney. Then there's our family friend, Jill, who has lost over twenty pounds this year through diet and exercise, and has a lovely dancer's physique due to her extensive dance background. (The Rockettes have got nothing on her!) I could look at those women and several others who are at the top of their game physically and think, *Wow, they have really arrived. They have got it all together. It must be nice to be at that level of fitness.*

But here's the thing—they may have "arrived," but in

order to stay at that level, they have to keep training. In other words, they had to train hard to get there, and they'll have to continue to put in the sweat equity to stay there. And I'm sure if you asked any of them, they'd tell you it wasn't an easy journey and that they still encounter dietary temptation, training injuries, busy schedules, and other day-to-day challenges that make it tough to stay in that kind of shape. It's not a onetime thing; it's a daily commitment.

They'd also tell you—it's worth it.

Guess what? It's the same thing in the spiritual realm. There are several "faith giants" whom I look up to and I think, *Wow, they've really arrived. They walk at such a high level of faith. They have really got it all together. It must be nice to be there.* But here's the thing—they, too, are daily attaining and growing in their relationship with God. If you asked any of them, they'd tell you that they are constantly pressing toward the goal, as Paul instructed in Philippians.

They still encounter problems. They still face illness. They still have family members who aren't serving God. They still experience financial difficulties. They still deal with the day-to-day stuff the devil throws at all of us. Plus, they have to deal with all of that in the public eye.

And they'd also tell you—it's worth it!

I recently heard one of them say, "If you ever think you've arrived spiritually, you're already in trouble." In other words, there's always more. There's always a deeper place with God. There's always more to learn from the Bible.

Maybe that's why the Word says that pride comes before a fall. If you ever think you've arrived spiritually and quit pressing toward the goal, the devil will be there to jerk that rug out from underneath your little feet. After that happens, the fall is sure to come. See, the enemy has only one goal—to kill, steal, and destroy. So if he sees an opening, he's taking it. Don't give him that opening. Don't be fooled into a false sense of security. If the apostle Paul felt that he needed to keep pressing on, I'm sure that all of us have some more growing to do.

Never be satisfied with your walk with God. Keep desiring more of Him. Keep learning more from His Word. Listen to more teaching podcasts and CDs. Spend more time meditating on His promises.

Keep on keeping on both physically and spiritually!

POWER PRAYER: *Father, help me to be inspired by both fitness and faith giants as I press toward my physical and spiritual goals. Help me, Lord, to never stop growing, learning, and attaining from glory to glory. In the Mighty Name of Your Son, Jesus, Amen.*

WORK YOUR WORDS: I will continue to grow and learn and attain both physically and spiritually. I will not become complacent.

HEALTHY HINT: Find a mentor! Find someone who is doing better than you in their fitness, healthy eating, serving God, etc. Follow that person on social media. Ask that person questions. Emulate your mentor. Let your mentor inspire you!

CHAPTER 35

TOO BLESSED TO BE STRESSED!

. . . .

"Are you tired? Worn out? Burned out on religion?
Come to me. Get away with me and you'll recover your life.
I'll show you how to take a real rest. Walk with me
and work with me—watch how I do it. Learn the unforced
rhythms of grace. I won't lay anything heavy or
ill-fitting on you. Keep company with me and
you'll learn to live freely and lightly."

Matthew 11:28–30 (MSG)

STRESS. IT CAN'T BE AVOIDED.

We all have those "I want to hide under my covers and eat bonbons" moments. Life can be super stressful. It's just a fact, but how we deal with that stress is what keeps us from being stressed out. And studies have shown that physical exercise is one of the best ways to combat stress. Not only does exercise reduce the body's stress hormones, such as adrenaline and cortisol, but exercise also increases your levels of endorphins, which are chemicals in the brain that act as natural mood boosters. In addition, regular exercise improves your body's ability to sleep well, which also reduces stress.

And there's more!

Exercise also provides emotional benefits, helping to decrease a person's overall stress. If you lose some of those unwanted pounds by working out, your strength, stamina, pride, confidence, and self-esteem will increase; thus, you'll feel better about yourself and life in general. Because, if we're honest, extra pounds can often keep us from stepping out in the things that God has for us to do.

I have a very close friend who confided in me that she had turned down several opportunities to speak at ladies' retreats simply because she was heavier than she had ever been. She said, "I feel like everyone is staring at how large my backside is, and it keeps me from ministering like I know I should." I couldn't believe what she was saying because she is one of the mightiest women of God that I know, and God had used her words to bless me so many times in my life. The truth is, God could use her at any weight, just the way she was, but she couldn't see it.

She was in tears as she admitted her paralyzing insecurity, and I cried right alongside her because I totally understood. The devil loves to use our insecurities against us and whisper in our ears that we're not good enough, that God could never use us, but the devil is a liar! Don't let the size of your backside keep you sidelined when God needs you in the game.

Speaking of games, exercise is a great diversion, so get out and "play." Join in a game of tag with your kiddos or grand-kids. Play some football in the park with your spouse and friends. Take a yoga class and feel that tension leave your body. Seriously, don't you always feel better—no matter how stress-ful the day has been—if you meet a friend after work to pound the pavement and vent? Exercise helps get your mind off your problems while engaging in healthy movement. It's a win/win.

While physical exercise is key to kicking stress right out of your life, it won't work alone. You also need to cast your cares on God. It's time to throw away those bonbons and come out from under the covers. God is the only covering you need! Start today confessing, "I am too blessed to be stressed," and begin to enjoy life.

POWER PRAYER: *Father, help me not to get overwhelmed with the daily stresses of life. Instead, help me to cast my cares and worries on You, Lord. And, Father, help me to turn to exercise and other healthy ways of dealing with stress. In the Mighty Name of Your Son, Jesus, Amen.*

WORK YOUR WORDS: I will find healthy ways to deal with my daily stress, and I purposely cast my cares on my Heavenly Father.

HEALTHY HINT: One very effective way to get rid of stress is through controlled, deep breathing. And the great thing about deep breathing is that you can do it in an office, in the car, or on an airplane—anywhere! Here are some deep breathing tips:

- Breathe in through your nose, and hold it for a count of five.
- Next, exhale through your mouth.
- Do this five times in a row, slowly and deliberately.

CHAPTER 36

ONLY GOD . . .

. . . .

Do not be carried away by varied and strange teachings;
for it is good for the heart to be strengthened by grace,
not by foods, through which those who
were so occupied were not benefited.

Hebrews 13:9 (NASB)

I RECENTLY READ a decorative wall hanging that said, "Why are you wasting time trying to fill a God-sized hole with sin-sized pieces?"

That's good, isn't it?

But you know what else we often try to fill that God-sized hole with?

Food.

They don't call it comfort food for nothing.

Even celebrities struggle with emotional eating. I recently read an article featuring an interview with Maria Shriver, who is a lovely, accomplished, powerful woman. Of all people, you wouldn't think she would have a weight problem, but she admitted that she has battled weight issues off and on her entire life. When asked about her struggle, she said, "Exercise is absolutely important, but I feel that people tend to overeat because they don't feel loved . . . someone who feels love often has a lot less issues with food."

Multitalented Wynona Judd has also been very honest about her battles of the bulge, even checking herself in to a rehab for food addiction in 2006. Regarding her emotional eating, she said in an interview: "I'd eat a box of doughnuts. It was like a chip, I couldn't eat just one. . . . I was eating thousands of calories each day."

She'd lose weight and then regain it and more. And when bad things happened in her life (such as when her marriage crumbled), she turned to food. Her life coach at the time, Dr. Ted Klontz, told *People* magazine, "Food made her feel better in her misery."

Of course, in the long run, food *didn't* make her feel better. It was simply a quick fix.

Maybe you can relate.

Emotional eating, which we use as a distraction from stress, sorrow, emptiness, pain, and boredom, is always a speedy satisfier but never a permanent solution. The reason we turn to food, even when we're not hungry, is because our souls are weary and discouraged, and food is tangible. Or, possibly, we associate food with pleasant memories so we automatically go back to what we know.

Whatever the reason for emotional eating, whenever you

find yourself going down that road, stop and think: *What am I really craving right now? Am I really craving ice cream, or am I truly craving something more permanent or satisfying?*

When we are able to identify that we're not really hungry for food but rather for God, we have won the battle. And as we practice this scenario each time we are tempted to emotionally eat an entire bag of cookies, we will get better at identifying the destructive pattern and overcoming it.

Whether your name is Maria, Wynona, or Michelle, the Word of God will work for you. God's Word never returns void! So grab hold of this scripture: "When you open your hand, you satisfy the hunger and thirst of every living thing" (Psalm 145:16, NLT).

Only God satisfies . . . can I get an amen?

POWER PRAYER: *Father, fill me up with Your love so that I won't need to overeat in order to be satisfied. I know that through You, I can do all things, so I believe that I will be able to overcome my tendencies to emotionally eat. I am excited that today I begin a new future with You—one that's free from emotional eating and bondage of any kind. I love You, Lord. In the Mighty Name of Your Son, Jesus, Amen.*

WORK YOUR WORDS: I will no longer crave food when I'm sad, depressed, angry, or bored. Instead, I will crave God and His love to fill up that emptiness.

HEALTHY HINT: There are several practical things you can do to counteract emotional eating.

Pray! And don't just pray in your head. Pray out loud a power prayer, such as: "Father, thank You for helping me resist the urge to give in to emotional eating. I am thankful that I can do all things—including overcoming this food addiction—through You."

Instead of reaching for that gallon of ice cream, reach for your phone and call a friend or a relative. Get the focus off of food and talk to a trusted person in your life about the real reason you are wanting to binge. Sometimes just talking through your emotions will be enough to get you past that urge to overeat.

Try journaling! Write your feelings, don't eat them. Write about anything and everything without holding back.

Do some deep breathing and stretching, or pop in a yoga DVD and clear your mind.

Sip some black tea! According to a study in the *Journal of Psychopharmacology*, people who drank black tea experienced a 47 percent drop in their cortisol levels, which is the stress hormone that makes you crave food.

CHAPTER 37

GOD'S GOT YOUR BACK

. . . .

Ye have not, because ye ask not.
James 4:2 (KJV)

I HAD BEEN ON THIS crazy book deadline for weeks, writing twelve to fourteen hours a day every day. As most writers, I am a creature of habit and I have a favorite place to write in my house. It's a room just off our kitchen with two walls of very large windows. And in the corner of that most perfect "office" is a comfy chair with a matching foot-stool, made especially for people with short legs. It's one of the only pieces of furniture we have that actually fits me. I can sit with my back all the way against the chair, and my feet still touch the floor. I love my writing spot. The problem is—my writing spot doesn't always love me.

After weeks of my bum being planted in the soft, comfy chair, my lower back started hurting so much that I could no longer sit anywhere. I had to stand at the kitchen counter to write. At night, when I tried to lie comfortably in bed, I could find no relief from the pain that started in the left side of my lower back and shot all the way down my left leg. I was miserable, and ibuprofen was no longer helping. Finally, I called a local chiropractor and explained what was going on. She told me to come right in, and after two times of meeting with her, I still had intense pain, sleepless nights, and a book deadline that I was trying desperately to meet.

While icing my back one afternoon, my cell phone rang— "Cecil Stokes." I smiled when I saw his name pop up on my phone, always happy to hear from my uber-talented writer/director/producer friend.

"Hey, how are you?" I asked.

"I'm great," he said, in his usual upbeat voice. "I have three really exciting things I need to talk to you about, but first, how are you?"

I paused for a moment, not wanting to be a "Connie Complainer," because I had so many wonderful tidbits of news I wanted to share with him since the last time we'd talked. But the pain got the best of me and I confessed, "Well, I'm a mess, actually . . . " and proceeded to tell Cecil all about my back situation and everything I'd been doing to try to rectify it.

He listened without interrupting and then very matter-of-factly asked, "So, I know this may be a silly question, but have you prayed for God to heal your back?"

Dead silence on the phone.

"Uhhhh, you know, I haven't done that," I answered, completely embarrassed. "That might be a good idea, huh?"

We both laughed.

"Would you pray for my back?" I asked my good friend and prayer warrior.

"I would love to pray for your back," Cecil said, and then he proceeded to do so.

And you know what? My back has been 100 percent better since that afternoon. I even worked out that same day, and I focused on my core because a strong core is important for a healthy back. (See the "Healthy Hint" below.)

The Bible says that we have not because we ask not (see James 4:2). So, why don't we ask? Why don't we go to God and ask for healing? In my case, I think I got caught up in the business of all I was trying to accomplish and simply tried to manage everything myself. I do that a lot; maybe you do, too.

I don't know what you're trying to manage right now, but let me tell you from someone who can speak from recent experience—asking God for His divine intervention is way better than trying to take care of everything on your own. Go ahead; ask for His help. If you need healing, God is the Great Physician. If you need peace, He has the peace that passes all understanding. If you need extra money so you can join your local gym, He owns the cattle on a thousand hills. If you need direction concerning healthy eating, He promises to order your steps. Whatever you're trying to handle on your own today, just give it to God. He has a promise with your name on it. He has the very answer you've been needing. So, ask! He's got your back—literally.

POWER PRAYER: *Father, I am asking You to get involved in every area of my life. I no longer want to manage things on my own. Thank You for leading me every step of the way and for having my back. In the Mighty Name of Your Son, Jesus, Amen.*

WORK YOUR WORDS: I will ask God for help in every area of my life. I will not try to manage things on my own without His guidance, His direction, or His wisdom.

HEALTHY HINT: More than 80 percent of Americans will suffer from back pain at some point in their lives due to a lack of activity and muscle atrophy. Strengthening your abdominals will prevent that from happening! In fact, the primary function of strong abs is not for aesthetics, it's to provide strength to your core and support for your back.

Here is one of my favorite core exercises—it's a Pilates basic. Lie on your back, hold the backs of your thighs, and pull your upper body toward your legs for an intense contraction. Then, reach your hands past your thighs for 100 tiny pulses and breaths.

CHAPTER 38

YO-YO? NO! NO!

. . . .

If any of you lacks wisdom, let him ask of God,
who gives to all liberally and without reproach,
and it will be given to him.

James 1:5 (NKJV)

OKAY, SO IT'S TIME to come clean with you. I am a repeat yo-yo diet offender. In fact, I have probably lost and gained the same fifteen pounds about a dozen times in my life. Dictionary.com defines *yo-yo dieting* as the practice of repeatedly losing weight by dieting and subsequently regaining it. You know how Albert Einstein defined it? Insanity! Which is doing the same thing over and over again and expecting different results.

Statistics reveal that more than 80 percent of people who have lost weight regain all of it or more after two years. Not very encouraging, is it? Not only is yo-yo dieting frustrating, but it's also dangerous for your health because the vicious cycle of losing weight and regaining it can result in high blood pressure, high cholesterol, cancer, diabetes, and depression. So why do we fall back into the same old patterns that caused us to gain weight in the first place?

Experts say that until we identify the trigger foods that cause us to regain the weight, we'll never be able to keep it off. For instance, I have identified a few trigger foods that I simply will not allow in my house. (Remember? I already admitted that those delectable white powdered doughnuts are my downfall.) But there are others, too. Every year when it gets close to Easter and the candy displays pop up in most every store, those ridiculously yummy Reese's Peanut Butter Eggs taunt me. I really love them, but I *never* buy them. Because if I buy a box of six, I'll eat two on the way home from the supermarket and probably finish off the rest before bedtime. No matter how hard I try, I can't stop myself. If white powdered doughnuts or Reese's eggs are around, I must eat them.

But here's what I learned from master personal trainer and nutritional counselor (as well as minister of the gospel) Marty Copeland when she shared from her heart at Eagle Mountain International Church in Fort Worth, Texas. (I took so many notes that day that my hand hurt!) She said that when she used to struggle with temptation in the form of her trigger foods, she applied the principle of sowing and reaping to that area of her life. So, for example, if she really desired a candy bar, she would only eat a few bites of it and leave the rest. Then she would say out loud, "I am resisting the temptation to eat this entire candy bar and I am sowing self-control to the Spirit." Eventually, she had sown enough self-control to the Spirit that she began living with a great measure of self-control. That's when she finally started succeeding in the battle of the bulge. She didn't learn that principle from the latest diet book; she learned it from the Word of God.

Isn't that good? God's Word and His ways work every time. You see, there is no true victory when you try to fight this battle with only the world's knowledge. Sure, you'll have some success, but not the kind of success that produces lasting results. Because even if you're able to drop a few pounds on some crazy fad diet, if you don't sow self-control to the Spirit and reprogram your thinking, the moment your diet is over, so is your success.

If you don't know what your trigger foods are, ask God to help you identify them so that you won't become a chronic yo-yo dieter. He wants to help, so just ask Him. And if those little white powdered sugar doughnuts aren't a trigger food for you, enjoy a couple in my honor. Ugh!

POWER PRAYER: *Father, I want You to get involved in my eating, and I praise You for giving me direction and discernment in this area. Help me to avoid those trigger foods, and Lord, please help me to sow self-control that I might reap a great harvest of it. Thank You for loving me. In the Mighty Name of Your Son, Jesus, Amen.*

WORK YOUR WORDS: I will make wise choices for my health, and I will not be part of the 80 percent who lose weight and gain it all back and then some after two years. I will succeed in attaining a healthy, fit body, because with God all things are possible!

HEALTHY HINT: Part of avoiding that whole yo-yo diet trap is simply making good dietary choices all throughout your day. However, if you don't have healthy snacks available, you might just opt for the quickest treat, which more than likely won't be the best option. So, here are seven healthy snacks to have on hand the next time you get hungry.

- Apple slices and a tablespoon of peanut butter for delicious dipping
- One fiber-packed tortilla with salsa
- Baked pumpkin seeds
- Half of an English muffin or a "skinny bagel" with veggie cream cheese
- Microwave popcorn (without the butter)
- Yogurt-covered raisins
- Hard-boiled eggs

CHAPTER 39

YOUR WORDS FRAME YOUR WORLD

. . . .

Take control of what I say, O LORD, and guard my lips.
Psalm 141:3 (NLT)

WHETHER OR NOT you know it, you are the prophet of your own life. You don't need to call the psychic hotline to find out what the future holds (you'd better not be doing that anyway); just listen to what you're saying and before long, you'll be living exactly what you're speaking. You've probably heard the old expression, "You are what you eat." But here's more truth: "You are what you say."

Our words hold creative power.

That's how it's been since the beginning of time. In fact, let's look at the first chapter of Genesis (NIV) together for further proof.

Genesis 1: In the beginning God created the heavens and the earth. Now the earth was formless and empty, darkness was over the surface of the deep, and the Spirit of God was hovering over the waters (v. 1).

And God said, "Let there be light," and there was light (v. 3).

And God said, "Let there be an expanse between the waters to separate water from water." So God made the expanse and separated the water under the expanse from the water above it. And it was so (vv. 6–7).

And God said, "Let the water under the sky be gathered to one place, and let dry ground appear." And it was so (v. 9).

Then God said, "Let the land produce vegetation: seed-bearing plants and trees on the land that bear fruit with seed in it, according to their various kinds." And it was so (v. 11).

And God said, "Let there be lights in the expanse of the sky to separate the day from the night, and let them serve as signs to mark seasons and days and years, and let them be lights in the expanse of the sky to give light on the earth." And it was so (vv. 14–15).

And God said, "Let the land produce living creatures according to their kinds: livestock, creatures that move along the ground, and wild animals, each according to its kind." And it was so (v. 24).

I could continue quoting verses here, but you get the idea. Notice any pattern here? *"And God said . . . and it was so."* This passage didn't say that "God thought" or that "God waved His hand over the earth . . . and it was so." No, it says, "God said."

See, God could've chosen any method to create this world,

but He chose to "speak" this world into existence, and you speak your world into existence, too, every single day.

So, what have you been saying? Be honest! Have you been saying things like, "I just can't lose weight"? Or, "I'll never be able to eat healthy; I just don't like vegetables"? Or, "I hate myself. I'm fat and I'll always be fat"? Or, "I hate working out. My body just doesn't move like that"? Or, "I'll always have a 'muffin top' so I might as well have another muffin"?

If you're guilty of uttering any of those statements, I feel for you. I've probably said several of those negative utterances myself at one time or another. But it's time to stop saying such negative comments! There really aren't any free words; every word we speak is important, because every word is a container, carrying either success or defeat. In fact, Proverbs 18:21 says this: "Words kill, words give life; they're either poison or fruit—you choose" (MSG).

You choose! Well, that's a no-brainer when you put it that way, isn't it?

Let's choose health. Let's choose happiness. Let's choose wholeness. Let's choose life!

POWER PRAYER: *Father, please put a watch over my words so that I will only say what You say about me. Help me to stop speaking negative things against myself and others. And, Lord, help me to "choose life" every day. In the Mighty Name of Your Son, Jesus, Amen.*

WORK YOUR WORDS: I will change my words; therefore, I will change my world.

HEALTHY HINT: Use your mouth to speak good things over yourself. Sometimes we have to speak by faith and call things that "be not" as though they were, amen? So get up every morning and say: "I am getting healthier and stronger every day, in every way!"

CHAPTER 40

YOUR GOALS ARE WITHIN REACH!

. . . .

Because we know that this extraordinary day is just ahead,
we pray for you all the time—pray that our God will make
you fit for what he's called you to be, pray that he'll fill
your good ideas and acts of faith with his own energy
so that it all amounts to something.

2 Thessalonians 1:11 (MSG)

ARE YOU AWARE that you already have everything you need to reach your goals?

It's true!

Having a healthy body may seem like only a dream. Wearing the size you have always hoped to wear may seem like an impossibility. Being able to run a 5K may seem like a ridiculous goal right now. But your goals are definitely within reach.

If you'll do the natural, God will show up and do the supernatural.

In other words, if you'll drink more water than soda; if you'll eat a grilled chicken salad instead of the burger and fries; if you'll walk a mile instead of lying on the couch watching TV all night; if you'll do what you can do in the natural, God will do the supernatural.

There are examples of this throughout the Bible. For instance, think about David. He was going to battle with the biggest, baddest giant in all the land, yet all he needed to defeat Goliath was a slingshot and five smooth stones. *How'd he kill that giant with just a slingshot and a stone?* you might wonder. Because God added the supernatural to David's natural.

The same could be said for Moses when he was leading God's people out of Egypt. You might remember the story. Moses lead the people to the edge of the Red Sea, and he had no idea what to do next. He knew Pharaoh's army was gaining on them and would be there soon. So Moses asked for direction from God, who instructed Moses to grab a stick, and lift it into the air. It was just an ordinary stick but when he lifted it into the air, God parted the sea and the Israelites walked across the dry land to the other side. God made the ordinary extraordinary.

See, you just have to do two things: Do what you know to do and trust God to do the rest. Can you do that?

Of course you can!

Even if you've failed at achieving these goals in the past, that doesn't mean you're going to fail this time. You've changed your mind-set. You're no longer using excuses to get out of eating healthy or keep you from being active. You're excited about your future. And your goals are not impossible to reach because you have Almighty God involved this time. So don't look at how many times you've failed before. Instead, rejoice because your dreams are about to manifest!

Whatever "giant" you're facing today, God will partner with you to destroy it—just like He did for David. And whatever bondage you need to escape from today, God will provide you with a way of escape, just like He did for Moses and the Israelites, even if He has to part the Red Sea to do so! He will go with you all the way!

Begin to praise God daily for His supernatural power, ability, and resources that will combine with your natural ability, actions, and strength and cause you to win. We can't help but succeed!

POWER PRAYER: *Father, with You, I know that all things are possible. I am excited that this time, things will be different; this time I will succeed because I have You partnering with me on this wellness journey. I am asking that You add Your supernatural with my natural, and Your extraordinary to my ordinary. I love You, God, and I'm so thankful for Your help and guidance in every area of my life. In the Mighty Name of Your Son, Jesus, Amen.*

WORK YOUR WORDS: With my natural efforts and God's power, we can do supernatural things together. No goal is out of reach.

HEALTHY HINT: Spices are one of nature's best kept health secrets. Just by adding a few spices to your smoothies and main dishes, you can improve your health in so many ways. So the next time you make a smoothie, why not try adding some cinnamon, nutmeg, allspice, or ginger? And the next time you are putting together a soup or pasta dish, try adding some turmeric, sage, rosemary, cilantro, red pepper, or oregano. Your body will thank you.

STRETCHING

. . . .

CHAPTER 41

WINNER OR WHINER?

. . . .

I can do all things through him who strengthens me.
Philippians 4:13 (ESV)

I HAD ONLY BEEN TEACHING the Fitness 101 class at my local gym for a few weeks when I decided to change it up a bit. Instead of setting my timer for thirty-second cardio circuit intervals, I decided to start with minute intervals. As I was setting up the gym for my class, putting mats and weights at the appropriate stations, I enthusiastically announced my plan to several of the ladies who were visiting with one another before class.

"Minute intervals?" one woman asked. "Oh, we only do thirty-second intervals . . . a minute would be too hard for us."

"Yeah, we never do minute intervals," another woman confirmed.

"Well, we are today," I replied, with a sly grin. "Trust me. You can do this."

But they weren't too sure. In fact, when I informed the rest of the class that we would be doing a minute's worth of exercise at each cardio station at least for the first time through the circuit, I heard several more complaints and a bit of whining. But that didn't stop me from proceeding with my plan, and you know what? They all did just fine—even better than fine! They didn't even flinch when asked to hold a plank for a minute, though I know their abs were on fire during those last fifteen seconds.

During cooldown that morning, I commented, "You guys whined a bit when we began today, but you also proved to yourselves that you are capable of doing so much more than you thought you could. You killed it on those minute intervals!"

They were all pretty proud of themselves, and I was proud of them too. That morning's fitness class with my favorite ladies got me to thinking—how many times do I whine to God when He is trying to stretch my faith? How many times do I fight with God when He is trying to move me to the next level?

More times than I care to admit, I concluded. I realized that I, too, am a bit of a whiner.

How about you? Are you in the "Whiners Club"?

A guest speaker recently visited our church, and his sermon's title was "Are You a Winner or a Whiner?"

Ouch.

Message received.

I think it's time for all of us to stop being whiners and embrace the winners we were all called to be. Because if we resist change and bellyache every time God stretches us or moves us a little out of our comfort zone, we will never know all that we're capable of accomplishing, and we may never achieve all that God has called us to do.

Let's determine today to be winners, not whiners.

Don't resist change. Don't fight with God when He tries to move you to the next level. Just go with it! I'm telling you what I told my Fitness 101 ladies: Trust me, you can do this! Better yet, trust Him! You can do this!

POWER PRAYER: *Father, help me to quit resisting change and embrace growth. I am excited about my future, Lord, and I know that You have a great plan for my life. Help me to step outside of my comfort zone—both spiritually and physically—and walk in all that You have for me. In the Mighty Name of Your Son, Jesus, Amen.*

WORK YOUR WORDS: I am a winner, not a whiner, and I am not afraid to step outside of my comfort zone—spiritually or physically. I can do all things through Christ who strengthens me.

HEALTHY HINT: If you've been walking a mile several times a week for several months, why not go for a mile and a half this week? Or try walking one lap, jogging one lap, and so on. If you've always used three-pound hand weights, reach for the five-pound weights this week. Or instead of doing three sets of eight reps, try doing three sets—fifteen, ten and then eight reps. Keep challenging yourself! Step outside of your comfort zone! (Of course, you'll want to check with your doctor before pushing it too hard—especially if you have any health conditions or injuries.)

CHAPTER 42

BUZZARDS SCHMUZZARDS

. . . .

And David was greatly distressed; for the people spake
of stoning him, because the soul of all the people was grieved,
every man for his sons and for his daughters: but David
encouraged himself in the LORD his God.

1 Samuel 30:6 (KJV)

I WAS JUST FINISHING the second-to-last lap of my three-mile jog, and I was definitely feeling the pain. Every pore in my body was sweating profusely. My face was red. And I was breathing pretty hard. It had been a few days since I'd run, and my body was like, *Hey, what are you doing? You're hurting me! Quit pushing so hard!*

As I pushed through the pain for the final lap, I noticed a big ol' buzzard circling overhead. I had to laugh. It was as if that buzzard had been watching me struggle—like a wounded animal—just waiting for me to drop dead. (I guess I must've looked worse than I felt!) At any rate, I was just stubborn enough to run the last lap even harder than I'd run the eleven previous laps. That buzzard wasn't about to discourage me from finishing that last mile.

So, have you seen any buzzards circling overhead lately? Buzzards come in many forms—negative bosses, disapproving spouses, critical friends, etc. A buzzard is anyone or anything that comes to discourage you and make you think you're not good enough. Some of you may have grown up in homes where your parents said derogatory things to you. Or maybe your significant other never encourages you. Or maybe you have a friend who is always around to offer a little dig that makes you feel less than capable. Or maybe you've encountered a buzzard or two at the gym in your pursuit of a healthy, fit body. No matter what form your buzzard comes in, be assured that he will come, and sometimes he brings his buzzard buddies. But you have to learn to ignore those buzzards; run your race, and encourage yourself in the Lord.

In the Bible, David had to encourage himself. He and his men had just returned home from a daunting battle to find their camp ravaged. Their wives and children had been captured by their enemies, and their camp had been burned. This was what you might call a very bad day. No doubt, David could feel the buzzards circling. Before long, his men turned on him and talked of stoning David. But David didn't give up. He didn't drop to the ground and say, "Okay, buzzards. You win, Have at it!" No, the Bible says that David encouraged himself in the Lord, meaning that he rehearsed the victories in his past and remembered how God had come through for him before. He chose to think about the goodness of God and His promises rather than focus on the desperation of the moment.

We can do the same thing in our everyday lives!

Guess what? Just seventy-two hours later, David and his men had regained their families and belongings, and David was named king.

Buzzards, schmuzzards. If you're feeling overwhelmed by those buzzards circling overhead, just encourage yourself in the Lord and keep on pressing toward your goals. Remind yourself of the many times when God has come through for you in the past. Mediate on His promises! Never give up! Just think what might happen in the next seventy-two hours . . .

POWER PRAYER: *Father, help me to ignore the buzzards in my life and instead focus on You and Your promises. Help me, Lord, to learn to encourage myself in You rather than become overwhelmed with negative circumstances. In the Mighty Name of Your Son, Jesus, Amen.*

WORK YOUR WORDS: I will not be deterred or discouraged by the buzzards in my life. I choose to encourage myself in the Lord!

HEALTHY HINT: If you've been struggling to increase your mileage, join the club. Here's how I've been gradually increasing my own. I walk one lap, jog one lap, walk one lap, jog one lap, and so on. You can also find several apps online that are designed to help you develop a run/walk program that improves your strength and stamina so you'll be able to run an entire 5K in just eight weeks of training.

CHAPTER 43

STEP OUT OF YOUR COMFORT ZONE

. . . .

"Have I not commanded you? Be strong and courageous.
Do not be terrified; do not be discouraged,
for the LORD your God will be with you wherever you go."

Joshua 1:9 (NIV)

LAST SUMMER, my youngest daughter, Allyson, mentioned that she thought her kitty, Madison, could use some company while she was in class all day at the Fashion Institute of Design & Merchandising (FIDM) in downtown LA. Her apartment was quite small, but plenty big enough for another feline, so we adopted a little boy kitten from a nearby shelter and named him Motley.

At first, Motley was the definition of "scaredy-cat," avoiding Madison, hiding when you talked to him, and only coming out from under the sofa for food and litter box breaks. But eventually, that little kitty warmed up to us and began exploring Ally's apartment—all three rooms.

Motley, Madison, and Ally lived in that small apartment,

keeping each other company, until she graduated from the FIDM this past March. Since then, Ally and her two kitties have been living in our Hoosier home back in Indiana while Ally pursues employment opportunities.

Of course, our home is much larger than Ally's LA apartment. In fact, her entire apartment could almost fit into our master bedroom suite, which is where you'll find Motley 24/7. Immediately, Madison made herself right at home, but not Mr. Motley.

He almost never leaves my bedroom and its familiar dimensions.

In an effort to get Motley out of his self-imposed confined quarters, I have carried him downstairs to spend time with the family and see what he is missing out on, but as soon as I put him down, he sprints back upstairs to his "kitty comfort zone."

The truth is, I'm not really that much different from Motley. There are times when I know God is trying to "carry me downstairs," urging me to "explore all that He has for me," and yet I am perfectly content to stay in my own little comfort zone. Like Motley, I feel safe there, so I simply stay in my self-imposed confined quarters. I find that I tend to do this in every area of my life—even when it comes to my workouts. For example, I have this one abs routine I do faithfully. I know it by heart, and I'm no longer being challenged by it. I have become comfortable in that abs workout, and I completely resist whenever my daughter, Ally, tries to add to it or switch it up on me. I even get a little belligerent.

Why do I resist? Fear that I won't be able to do a new routine. Fear that it might hurt too much. Fear that I'll embarrass myself if I can't do the new abdominal exercises full-out because I'm not "in shape" enough. So basically—fear.

I'm truly just like Motley.

My comfort zone may feel safe, but it's actually a very dangerous place to dwell because it's keeping me from God's best. When we get too comfortable in the physical realm—specifically in our workouts—it can delay our progress indefinitely. You see, our muscles need us to "change it up" and find other ways to work them so that they stay challenged. The workout world calls it "Muscle Confusion."

And when we get too comfortable, spiritually speaking, it also keeps us from God's best. We aren't able to walk in all that God has for us, or do all that He desires to accomplish through us.

I'm hoping that one day soon, Motley will venture out into other parts of the house and take advantage of the morning sun in our sunroom, as well as spend time with the family in our living room. I know he will love both! And I'm happy to report that I have downloaded some new abdominal workouts that I will be implementing into my old tried-and-true routine.

I imagine God is hoping we step out of our comfort zones,

spiritually speaking, as well. Not only does He have work for us to do, but He also has blessings awaiting us if we'll only follow Him. So, c'mon, all you "comfortable cats," let's step out of our comfort zones today.

POWER PRAYER: *Father, help me to step out of my comfort zone—both physically and spiritually. I trust You, Lord, and I want Your best in every area of my life. I give all of my fears to You. In the Mighty Name of Your Son, Jesus, Amen.*

WORK YOUR WORDS: I will not be afraid! I will step out of my comfort zone, and I will follow God in every area of my life.

HEALTHY HINT: If you always walk three miles on the treadmill, why not step off the treadmill and try thirty minutes on the stair climber or the elliptical machine instead? Or if you've been doing the exact same three sets, using the exact same amount of weight for a while, why not vary it a bit this week? Do more reps or increase the weight!

CHAPTER 44

DO YOU HAVE A FOCAL POINT?

. . . .

And let us run with endurance the race
God has set before us. We do this by keeping our eyes on Jesus,
the champion who initiates and perfects our faith.

Hebrews 12:1b–2a (NLT)

AT THE END of every fitness class I teach—whether it's a cardio dance session or a Fitness 101 class—I end with a cooldown. During this portion of the class, I play softer, slower, inspiring music, and we take time to stretch. I love it. It's a perfect time to work on flexibility since the muscles are already warm, so we do several positions of static stretching. It's all very peaceful and enjoyable until we get to the quadriceps stretch (of the large muscles in the front of the thigh). That's when I ask the ladies to either go to a wall for balance or find a focal point in the room in order to execute the stretch without falling over. As you probably know, the proper way to stretch your quads, while in a standing position, is to grab one foot and pull the leg behind while balancing on the other leg, and this requires some coordination and balance. I always remind my ladies to bend the knee of the supporting leg, which will help keep them stable while stretching, and I continue encouraging them to look at their individual focal points. However, sometimes as I'm coaching them, I'm doing so while hopping around on my own like a hot mess. Some days my balance is just better than others—not sure why—but I have to admit there are times when I have trouble balancing long enough to get a stretch in before falling over. Ever been there?

But even on those days, if I truly find a focal point on the gym floor or on the mirrored wall, and keep my eyes there throughout the remainder of the stretch, I don't wobble nearly as much. Instead, I can hold the stretch with strength and balance.

It's much the same way in our spiritual lives, if you really think about it. When we take our eyes off of Jesus, we become completely off-balance and wobble through life, always on the brink of falling down. In other words, we're hot messes. But when we stay focused on Jesus, everything else falls into place, and we can lead happy, healthy, whole, balanced lives.

It's just like the Scriptures say: We can run the race set before us if we keep our eyes on Jesus, the champion who initiates and perfects our faith. Can I hear an amen? When we stay focused on Jesus, we can stand firm even when others are wobbling all around us. So keep your eyes on Him and move through life with confidence, stability, balance, and strength.

(Oh, and if you're having a "hot mess" kind of day—don't worry. He loves us on those days, too.)

POWER PRAYER: *Father, help me to keep my eyes on Jesus— no matter what. And, help me, Lord, to never lose sight of my physical and spiritual goals. Keep me from being a hot mess, Lord, and help me to stay focused and balanced and strong so that I can fulfill my calling. In the Mighty Name of Your Son, Jesus, Amen.*

WORK YOUR WORDS: I will keep my eyes on Jesus and live a well-balanced, healthy, and happy life.

HEALTHY HINT: It's always a great idea to work on your flexibility at the end of a workout when your muscles are already warm, because they are more elastic at that time. Stretching a cold muscle could result in injury, so always take a few minutes to lightly warm up before stretching.

CHAPTER 45

MISPLACED PRIORITIES . . .

. . . .

Since, then, you have been raised with Christ,
set your hearts on things above, where Christ is
seated at the right hand of God. Set your minds
on things above, not on earthly things.

Colossians 3:1–2 (NIV)

YOU'VE PROBABLY SEEN those Facebook posts or Twitter tweets from the gym rats who say things like, "If the gym were a church, and lifting was a religion, I'd be the holiest person in the world." Or, "Who needs church when my 'temple' looks this good?" (You're cringing a bit as you read those, aren't you? Don't worry; so did I!)

Yep, you might say the authors of those social media blurbs might have their priorities a bit out of whack, or possibly a lot out of order. While it's wonderful to strive for a healthy, fit body, if working out consumes your thoughts and takes up most of your time, the gym has become an idol in your life.

Let's approach this like Jeff Foxworthy of the "You might be a redneck if . . . " brand.

You might have misplaced priorities if . . .

- Your quest for a lean body has you researching all the best ways to shred online while neglecting your devotional time.
- You'd rather skip church than a workout.
- Most of your time, money, and energy is spent in your quest for a perfect body.
- All the apps on your smartphone have to do with diet and fitness (and there's not one Bible or devotional app).
- You are more excited to talk about the best protein shakes than the things of God.
- You put your new bumper sticker, "Living to Lift" over the top of your earlier "Got God?" bumper sticker.

Yes, I'm having a little fun here, but seriously, we have to get our priorities straight if we want to succeed in every area of life, and that means giving God the top spot. You see, the Bible says that God is a jealous God. He wants to be first place in our lives, but He is also a gentleman. He won't barge His way into our lives. We have to seek Him, and seeking requires time.

Matthew 6:33 says, "But seek first the kingdom of God and His righteousness, and all these things shall be added to you" (NKJV).

Dictionary.com defines *seek* as: "to go in search or quest of; to try to find or discover by searching or questioning; to follow or pursue."

So insert those phrases into the above scripture to get a clear meaning of what "seeking God" really means. For example, "But *pursue* first the kingdom of God and His righteousness, and all these things shall be added to you."

Why do you think He wants us to seek Him?

Because God's way always works! When we desire for God to reveal Himself so much that we put Him before other things, we will experience the things of God in a way we've never known and enjoy a peaceful, happy, balanced life.

So, determine today to redirect your attention to God. Give Him first place, and everything else will fall into place. Let Him order your day. Include Him in your planning. Seek Him, and when you do that, your misplaced priorities will be properly ordered.

POWER PRAYER: *Father, I repent for not putting You first every single day, and I ask that You help me to get my priorities straight. I love You, Lord, and I purposely set my affections on You today and forevermore. Thank You for going with me on this fitness and weight-loss journey. In the Mighty Name of Your Son, Jesus, Amen.*

WORK YOUR WORDS: I will put You first, God, today and every day.

HEALTHY HINT: Ask God to help you organize your life and keep your priorities straight, and He will. While it's not good to obsess over working out, it's also not good to ignore fitness altogether. Find a healthy balance. You might even combine the two—get up and have your devotions while riding the exercise bike, or go on a prayer walk.

CHAPTER 46

ENLARGE YOUR CIRCLE

. . . .

My dear friends, in the name of the Lord Jesus,
I beg you not to have anything to do with any of your people
who loaf around and refuse to obey the instructions
we gave you. You surely know that you should follow
our example. We didn't waste our time loafing.

2 Thessalonians 3:6–7 (CEV)

I RECENTLY READ A QUOTE from T. D. Jakes that made a lot of sense to me. He said, "If you're the smartest person in your circle, you're in the wrong circle—you've outgrown it. It's time to move to the next level."

I've also heard a version of this quote used in business settings, encouraging people to challenge themselves by hanging out with entrepreneurs who are more driven and experienced than they are.

But I had yet another version of this quote spoken directly to me from my daughter's boyfriend this past week. Ally, Wes, and I have been hitting the Milwaukee Trail (a popular place to walk, jog, hike, and bike in our neck of the woods) the past few months, and just recently we've all been training for upcoming races. I'm going to do another 5K (I haven't run a 5K in two years), and Ally and Wes are going to do the Tough Mudder, which is a ten- to twelve-mile obstacle course that is designed to test physical strength and mental grit. (They don't call it "Tough" Mudder for nothing!)

Obviously, their training is way more intense than mine, but last week when I accompanied them, Wes said, "You should train with us!"

"I thought I was," I answered.

"No," he continued, "you should train *with* us."

"You mean, do what you're doing?" I asked, with a pained look on my face.

"Exactly," he answered. "You can do it! You just need someone to push you."

As much as I hated to admit it, he was right.

I always accompanied the training twosome to the Trail, but I also always let them run ahead of me, content to walk at my own comfortable pace. But that was the problem—I'd grown too comfortable with my training. I hadn't been pushing myself. Ever since I'd had gallbladder surgery the previous April, I'd been a little nervous about running again.

Afraid it might hurt.

Afraid I might not be able to run like I had before.

Afraid to even try . . . until that night when Wes pushed me into it.

Guess what? He was right! I was able to run—only about

five minutes at a time before I had to walk again—but it was a start. And that start was all I needed to get back at it—no longer afraid to train harder.

I had enlarged my "training circle" to include Wesley, and he wasn't afraid to push me. (I might add that he continues to push me, which is a good thing. He and Ally are either going to kill me or make me better!)

So, how are the circles in your life? Are you being challenged in every area of your life, or are you very comfortable these days, not being stretched at all? If you're the smartest one, the fittest one, the most inspiring one in your circle, then it's time to get a new circle or at least add to your existing ones.

POWER PRAYER: *Father, help me to step outside of my comfort zone and enlarge my circle. And, Lord, please bring new people into my life who will draw me closer to You, closer to my goals, and closer to the destiny that You have for me. In the Mighty Name of Your Son, Jesus, Amen.*

WORK YOUR WORDS: I will step out of my comfort zone and enlarge my circle so that I will remain challenged.

HEALTHY HINT: If you have a smartphone, there are so many apps that will nudge you right out of your training comfort zone. If you're training for a 5K like I am, download the free app c25K, and at the end of eight weeks, you'll be ready to run! The program is designed to take you from the couch to running a 5K—whoo-hoo! Alternating walking and running, you work out three times a week, for thirty to fourty minutes, building your endurance and your strength. There are numerous success stories from those who have used this program, so check it out!

CHAPTER 47

REST UP!

. . . .

"And when they sleep, they will wake up refreshed."
Jeremiah 31:26 (CEV)

LET ME ASK YOU SOMETHING . . . are you getting enough sleep?

Probably not, if you're like most women today.

Millions of people who live in this fast-paced world get six or fewer hours of sleep each night—and that is not enough, according to Dr. James B. Maas, author of *Power Sleep* (HarperCollins, 1999).

It seems that Americans have become too busy to sleep, and we're suffering the consequences. Deprivation of sleep can cause many problems, including: daytime drowsiness; mood shifts; depression; increased irritability; loss of sense of humor; stress anxiety; loss of coping skills; loss of interest in socializing with others; feelings of being chilled; reduced immunity to disease and viral infection; feelings of lethargy; reduced productivity; reduced ability to concentrate; reduced ability to remember; reduced ability to handle complex tasks; reduced ability to think logically; decreased ability to assimilate and analyze new information; reduced ability to think critically; reduced decision-making skills; decreased vocabulary and communication skills; reduced creativity; reduced motor skills and coordination; decreased perceptual skills, and weight gain.

Yes, weight gain.

Ever pulled an all-nighter to complete a paper, help your child with a homework assignment, or finish wallpapering a room, and find yourself elbow-deep in a potato chip bag about 2 a.m.? Well, you're not alone. Studies have shown that when you're sleepy, you're 50 percent more likely to experience powerful cravings for carbs. (I can personally attest to that, having pulled many all-nighters over the course of my career in order to hit deadlines, and devouring bags and bags of Peanut M&M's to make it through, haha!)

Bottom line: We need sleep. It affects every aspect of our day-to-day living. In fact, it's as important to our overall well-being as healthy eating and exercising.

Not only do we need to make physical rest a priority, but we also need to make spiritual rest a priority. Psalm 23 says: "The LORD is my shepherd; I have all that I need. He lets me rest in green meadows; he leads me beside peaceful streams. He renews my strength" (vv. 1-3 NLT).

So, how long has it been since you've rested in green meadows? My guess is—too long! Pastor Joel Osteen of Lakewood Church in Houston, Texas, says that he has to have a few minutes in his recliner each day to simply meditate on the goodness of God. Without those minutes of just sitting before God, he feels out of balance.

I can relate; how about you?

If we don't take time to just sit before God and meditate on His goodness and His promises, we might spin our wheels all day long and accomplish nothing.

But you say, "Michelle, I have my daily devotional time each morning. I read one chapter of the Bible, along with a devotional entry, and I pray for fifteen minutes. I'm doing fine!" My response is this—you are doing great! Those things are very important, but if your prayer life is like mine, I spend most of my time praying for everyone on my prayer list, thanking God for loving me, and then call it good. I rarely just sit in His presence and rest in Him.

We need that green meadow time. Make a conscious decision today to rest in Him. Find a few minutes to bask in His glory. Pencil in "green meadow" time in your daily planner, and stick to it. God is waiting . . . (P.S.: Sneak in a nap today, too, if you can!)

POWER PRAYER: *Father, I am so thankful that I can rest in You, both physically and spiritually. Help me not to stress out over things that I shouldn't, and help me learn to cast my anxieties on You. I trust You, Lord. In the Mighty Name of Your Son, Jesus, Amen.*

WORK YOUR WORDS: I rest in You, Lord, both physically and spiritually. Thank You for sweet sleep.

HEALTHY HINT: If you can squeeze in a nap, try to do so before lunch so that it doesn't interfere with your sleep schedule at night. Also, limit your nap to no more than thirty minutes. Power naps are awesome! You'll wake up rejuvenated and ready for the rest of the day.

CHAPTER 48

DON'T BUY THE LIE

For God is working in you, giving you the desire and the power to do what pleases him.

Philippians 2:13 (NLT)

I HAD JUST FINISHED TEACHING my Fitness 101 class when I overheard a woman discussing joining the gym with one of my fellow trainers. A rather large woman, I could tell she felt out of place in the gym just by her body language, so I decided to do what I could to make her feel welcome. I introduced myself and told her that I was one of the fitness instructors and that I'd love to have her join me in class sometime.

Without even making eye contact with me, she said: "Well, I appreciate that, but I doubt I'll end up joining. I've always been big. My mom was big. My sister's big. I honestly don't know why I'm trying to fight it. I'll probably always be big."

I didn't know whether to hug her, encourage her, or just shake her really good.

She had obviously bought the lie.

"What lie?" you ask.

The lie that the enemy tries to use against all of us—that we just need to be satisfied right where we are because it'll never get any better than this.

Stupid devil.

Here's the deal: The devil is the father of all lies, so you can't believe any thought he puts into your mind. If he is telling you that you're always going to be big because your entire family is big, say out loud: "No, I won't, devil, because I am breaking this family curse of obesity. It stops with me! With God, all things are possible! I will be healthy, happy, and whole, and there's not a thing you can do about it!"

We don't serve a status quo kind of God. He wants the very best for us, so why should we settle for any less? It's time we take the limits off of God and allow Him to do big things in us and through us. We have to stop thinking so small. We can't be content with mediocrity when God has put greatness on the inside of every one of us. I'm praying that as you read this, a fire of faith begins burning up that attitude of mediocrity that might've taken root in your heart over the years.

Maybe you don't see yourself as capable. Maybe you've simply accepted the status quo, but think of this: We serve Almighty God, the Creator of the Universe, and you are His child. He created us in His image, which means we have the blueprint of greatness, amen!

If you can relate to the woman I encountered at the gym, stuck in the status quo, afraid to believe for anything better, then today is your day to step out in faith! Get healthy, not for vain reasons, but for God reasons. Once you start pursuing wellness because you long to be a better vessel for Him, the journey becomes less about the number on the scale and more about God. You'll begin realizing that it's not about losing weight; it's about getting healthy so you can do God's work and enjoy the life He has given you. If you're committed to do what He wants you to do, He will help you accomplish your goals.

POWER PRAYER: *Father, thank You for seeing more in me than I see in myself. I believe that You have created me for a divine purpose, and I long to be in my best health to carry out that mission. Thank You for helping me become the best version of me. In the Mighty Name of Your Son, Jesus. Amen.*

WORK YOUR WORDS: I will not be satisfied with the status quo. I believe that God will see to it that I am healthy and whole and able to fulfill the work He has planned for me.

HEALTHY HINT: Try never to go grocery shopping on an empty stomach. If you shop hungry, you're more likely to make impulse buys of cookies, crackers, etc. Go armed with a list of foods that are on your healthy eating plan, and don't stray from that list. If you don't buy it, you can't eat it. It's as simple as that.

CHAPTER 49

THE REAL DEAL ON THE MEAL DEAL

. . . .

So whether you eat or drink, or whatever you do,
do it all for the glory of God.

1 Corinthians 10:31 (NLT)

"WELCOME TO BURGERLAND. May I take your order?"

"Yes, I'll have a cheeseburger, small fries, and a small Coke."

As you're waiting for your total, the voice comes back over the speaker and tempts, "For a limited time, you can supersize your fries and drink for only thirty-nine cents more. Would you like to do that today?"

For only thirty-nine cents more I can have twice the fries and soda. What a deal!

"Sure," you answer, proud of yourself for being such a wise consumer. But just how wise were you? Let's investigate how much this quick decision will cost you in the long run.

- Your original order: a cheeseburger (330 calories and 14 fat grams), small fries (210 calories and 10 fat grams), and a small 16-ounce Coke (180 calories and 0 fat grams).

- Your supersize order: a cheeseburger (330 calories and 14 fat grams), supersize fries (610 calories and 29 fat grams), and a 32-ounce supersize Coke (360 calories and 0 fat grams).
- The difference? A whopping 580 calories and 19 fat grams!
- Over a year's time, if you opted for the supersized deal three times a week, that would amount to an extra 90,480 calories and an added 2,964 fat grams, resulting in approximately 26 extra pounds (based on the formula that each pound is made up of 3,500 calories and you did nothing extra to burn off any of the added calories).

No matter how you look at it, that's scary!

What can we learn from this scenario?

Just say no!

Yes, we want to be good consumers, but don't let that value-system mentality con you into buying more food. If you're sacrificing your health to save money, that's not using wisdom. Yet we are presented this scenario all the time. The last time Jeff and I went to the movies, I ordered a medium drink and the young man behind the counter said, "For twenty-five cents more, you can get a large with free refills."

I kid you not, that large cup looked like a mini swimming

pool. I have no idea how many ounces were actually in the cup, but it was way too many. I simply said, "No, thank you." It was as easy as that.

You can do the same!

In order to live a healthier lifestyle, we also must learn to identify a "normal-sized portion" and apply that knowledge when we go out to eat. For example, an appropriate serving size of meat is 2 to 4 ounces, which is about the size of a deck of cards. An appropriate serving of vegetables is a half cup, which is about the size of a light bulb. And an appropriate serving of fruit is about the size of a tennis ball.

So, with the appropriate serving sizes in mind, you can easily decide if the portions on your plate at the restaurant are too large. Chances are, they will be. Over the past two decades, serving sizes have increased dramatically, and so have our waistlines. So, here's a great solution to the portion problem. Ask the server to split your meal onto two plates and share dinner with your friend, significant other, child, etc. Most servers are happy to do that for you in the kitchen. If, by chance, you're dining alone or nobody at your table wishes to split a meal, then only eat half of what is on your plate and take home the rest in a doggie bag. (Can anyone say, "Lunch tomorrow"? Yay!)

You may be thinking, *Michelle, you've gone from ministering to meddling. Leave my portion sizes alone!* Well, I understand your frustration, and I'm not saying you have to get a kids' meal (though I often do, because they are enough!). I'm just saying that God wants us to make better choices, like eating in moderation, not for His benefit, but for ours.

Bottom line: God only gave us one body, and He expects us to take good care of it so that we can live healthy, whole, happy lives and accomplish all that He has for us. When you put it like that, all of that "meal dealing" doesn't really sound that appealing, does it?

POWER PRAYER: *Father, help me to better identify serving sizes and make better decisions concerning my eating. Lord, I am thankful to be alive. Help me, God, to take good care of this body You've given me. In the Mighty Name of Your Son, Jesus, Amen.*

WORK YOUR WORDS: I will not fall for the super-size meal deals. Instead, I will make decisions that are better for my health because I'm worth it.

HEALTHY HINT: If you'd like to learn more about the topic of healthy eating and portion control when eating out, you might want to check out these books written by Hope Warshaw, a registered dietitian. They are: *Guide to Healthy Restaurant Eating* (American Diabetes Association, 2009) and *The Restaurant Companion: A Guide to Healthy Eating Out* (Surrey Books, 1995).

CHAPTER 50

GET THE RIGHT PERSPECTIVE

· ·

I will praise the LORD at all times.
I will constantly speak his praises.

Psalm 34:1 (NLT)

MY LATE MAMA, Marion Medlock, used to always say, "If you complain, you'll remain, but if you praise, you'll be raised." That saying may not have originated with her, but she said it so many times throughout her life that I was sure she was the author.

My mama had such a grateful heart, and of all her wonderful qualities, I think that's the one I admired the most. She taught us to be thankful and to see the good in every situation. In other words, she taught us to keep the right perspective.

What an important lesson! You see, if we have the right perspective as we go through life, we won't just endure life; we'll enjoy it! And, yes, you can even enjoy this season of getting healthy. I know, it seems crazy to say that you'll actually enjoy doing cardio (do you have one of those shirts that says,

"Don't put me down for cardio"? haha), but you will! Here's how: Instead of complaining that you have to walk a mile at the track tonight, rejoice over the fact that you have the ability to walk! Celebrate that you have two working legs! If you're meeting a friend at the track, thank God for a fitness friend to log the miles with you.

Bottom line: You can always find a reason to be grateful.

First Thessalonians 5:18 says that we should give thanks in all circumstances. It doesn't say we should be thankful *for* the bad circumstances, but rather *in spite* of them.

So, when you face challenges on this road to wellness, don't complain about those obstacles. Instead, take a moment to praise God that He is on this journey with you. Praise Him that He promises to never leave you or forsake you. Praise Him because no challenge is too big for Him. Praise Him because you know that with Almighty God in your corner, you can accomplish anything, because nothing is too big for our God!

I realize that it's easy to lose that grateful attitude when we feel like we're just going through the motions of life—doing the same things, going the same places, seeing the same people, eating the same foods, working the same job, etc. But we must be careful that, in all of our "mundaneness," we don't lose sight of the wonder of life or fail to recognize the joy of the season that we're in right now.

You may be in that kind of rut right now, but you don't have to stay there. You can choose today to praise God and be purposefully grateful.

You might be thinking, *Michelle, I'm glad you can find a reason to be thankful, but I can't think of anything to be grateful for today. My life is a mess.*

Well, let me help you.

- Praise Him for the breath in your lungs.
- Praise Him for your family and friends.
- Praise Him that you have a job to go to every morning. (Or, if you don't have a job right now, praise God for the one He has for you down the road.)
- Praise Him for His unconditional love and His mercies that are new every morning!
- Praise Him for a roof over your head!
- Praise Him that you are physically able to work out.
- Just praise Him!

You'll soon discover that seeds of discouragement cannot take root in a grateful heart. So instead of looking at what's wrong in your life, why don't you thank God for what's right? Instead of dwelling on how far you've got to go, thank God for how far you've already come!

There are 1,440 minutes in every day . . . don't waste even one complaining. Appreciate the gift of today.

POWER PRAYER: *Thank You, Heavenly Father, for the gift of today. Help me, Lord, not to waste even one minute complaining. Keep my perspective right, Father, and help me to always have a grateful heart. I love You. In the Mighty Name of Your Son, Jesus, Amen.*

WORK YOUR WORDS: I am thankful for another day to live and love! Every day is a gift from God, so I will make the most of every minute!

HEALTHY HINT: Make a list of five things you can be grateful for today and post that list someplace where you will see it every day. Then read over that list several times every morning and thank God for those blessings. Every week, add one or two more things you're grateful for. As your list grows bigger, so will your joy level!

CHAPTER 51

A CLEANSE DOES
A BODY GOOD

· ·

But if we confess our sins to him,
he is faithful and just to forgive us our sins
and to cleanse us from all wickedness.

1 John 1:9 (NLT)

I REACHED INTO OUR FRIDGE to grab the carton of egg whites, and when I did, I totally knocked over an open can of soda.

Grape soda.

As you might imagine, it was sticky and messy and purple and all over everything. So I had to remove everything from the shelves and wipe each item to remove the grape sticky substance, and then I had to clean all of the shelves, too. (Did I mention this was first thing in the morning, like before I'd had any caffeine?) This was not the way I wanted to start my morning, but you know what? Once I cleaned up the grape soda fiasco, I discovered several of the food items I was about to put back into my nice clean fridge had already expired, so I tossed them.

This "cleansing" also inspired me to clean out the vegetable and fruit drawers. Turns out, they were somewhat yucky too. After about two hours of cleaning and throwing out stuff, I had a very clean, very functional refrigerator, and I was very happy with the end result. Of course, the cleaning process itself hadn't been so fun, but the end result made it all worth it.

You know, we need to go through "cleanses," too, both physically and spiritually. In fact, some experts suggest four cleanses per year in order to rid our bodies of toxins (aka, yucky stuff). I'm not talking about the "two-day miracle juice cleanses" that guarantee a twelve-pound weight loss in a weekend. I'm talking about the ones that truly rid your body of unwanted toxins and candida buildup.

I had to do a liver cleanse this past year before and after my gallbladder surgery. The doctor-supervised cleanse that I went on lasted only three days, but those were an intense three days! The first day, I thought my head was going to explode it hurt so badly. The doctor assured me that was very normal and just a part of the cleansing process. He encouraged me, "Just keep on the program and at the end of day three, you will feel so much better."

I followed his advice and toughed it out, and you know what? He was right! I did feel better physically. I had way more energy. My complexion was glowing. (My sister said I even looked younger!) And I had real mental clarity. My conclusion? Cleansing is a game changer! Just make sure that you go on a doctor-approved cleanse and do exactly what it says for as long as it says.

But you know what's even better? A spiritual cleansing.

If you've been away from God or sort of walking the fence between living for Him and living for the world, it's time for a spiritual cleanse. Here's the good news: You don't have to drink a lemon juice, cayenne pepper, and maple syrup concoction for it to work; you simply have to bask in your Heavenly Father's presence. Repent of your waywardness and ask Him to fill you up with His love, His peace, and His goodness, removing all sin (aka, yucky stuff) from your heart. This "Kingdom Cleanse" is the best cleanse ever!

So, go ahead, girl! Get your cleanse on!

POWER PRAYER: *Thank You, Heavenly Father, for Your never-ending grace. I am asking that You forgive me of my sins and cleanse me from all unrighteousness. And, Lord, fill me up with more of Your love, Your peace, and Your goodness so that I might be more like You. Also, Lord, I am asking for wisdom when choosing the right cleanse for my physical body, and the strength to carry it through. In the Mighty Name of Your Son, Jesus, Amen.*

WORK YOUR WORDS: I believe it's time for a cleansing in every area of my life, and I can't wait to celebrate the end results.

HEALTHY HINT: Many experts suggest doing a cleanse before embarking on a new healthy way of eating. You know, to sort of clean out your system—a system reboot—before changing up your eating habits.

Not sure whether you need to cleanse? Well, if you have any of the following symptoms on a regular basis, your body is probably in dire need of a reboot. (But remember, I went on a *doctor-supervised* cleanse. You'll want to check with your personal physician before committing to a cleanse. So, don't just go to your local health food store and buy the latest, greatest cleanse . . . check with your doctor first.)

1. You have trouble losing weight no matter what you do.
2. You often experience digestion problems, especially constipation.
3. You have trouble sleeping.
4. You have skin problems and allergic reactions.
5. You are tired all the time, no matter how many naps you take throughout the day.

CHAPTER 52

WILL IT 'TIL YOU FEEL IT!

. . . .

I take joy in doing your will, my God,
for your instructions are written on my heart.
Psalm 40:8 (NLT)

MY PASTOR RECENTLY SHARED a sermon about wanting to know God's will for your life, and then wanting to do God's will once you know what it is He desires for you to do.

In other words, it's not enough to know God's will. That's just the first step. We have to know the will of God and then go forward with that knowledge to carry out His plans for us.

He went on to say that if you don't know God's will for your life; if you really need to hear from Him; if you really need answers to any question—open God's Word and begin reading it on a regular basis. Everything you'll ever need to know is in the Bible.

"But here's the thing," he added. "The Word of God is like a can of paint. It only has value if we open it up and apply it."

That's good, isn't it?

See, you can read the Word of God and memorize large chunks of scripture, but if you don't apply what the Bible says to your life, it accomplishes nothing. That paint inside the can might be the loveliest shade of yellow ever, but if you don't dip your paintbrush in it and begin brushing it onto your walls, it serves no purpose.

You know what else is like that?

Your wellness plan.

You can research the amount of calories a person of your height and age and activity level should consume each day. And you can know that you should be drinking at least 64 ounces of water each day. And you can understand the importance of eating organic foods and avoiding processed ones. And you can believe that it's important to add more movement into your daily life. But until you actually apply that knowledge to your life, and begin doing those things you know you should do, then you're not going to see any results. You'll just simply stay the same way and never take any steps forward on your wellness path.

So, are you with me? Are you determined to know God's will for your life and then execute it accordingly? And are you willing to discover the best wellness plan for you and then apply it to your daily life?

Good! Then, that leads me to this last important point: You should want to do all of this. You see, eventually God wants to move some stuff out of the "duty column" and into the "desire column." And you can't wait until you *feel* like changing or implementing these important directives into your life; instead, you have to *will* it until you *feel* it. You've probably heard the expression, "Fake it 'til you make it." Well, that's what I'm saying to do as you begin getting healthy—spiritually and physically.

In other words, you may not feel like reading the Word of God, but as you delve into God's Word and bask in His presence, you'll begin to look forward to your quiet time with Him. And though you may not feel like drinking another glass of water, do it, because you know you're supposed to and eventually, your body will begin craving H_2O.

Knowing God's will is one thing. Doing God's will is quite another. And doing God's will with a good attitude—not out of obligation, but out of servitude—well, that's the icing on the cake. That should be our goal. When we can do those three things, we will be fulfilled in every way, thriving in every area of our lives.

POWER PRAYER: *Father, please reveal Your will for my life, and help me to want to carry out the plans that You have for me. Create in me an enthusiastic and willing heart, God, and help me to desire Your will in every area of my life. In the Mighty Name of Your Son, Jesus, Amen.*

WORK YOUR WORDS: I not only know the will of God for my life, but I am also actively pursuing it every day in every area of my life.

HEALTHY HINT: Sometimes it helps to have a workbook or a food journal to record your progress and write down your victories and defeats. For example, if I am keeping track of my meals and snacks every day, I can compare my food intake on the days when I see weight loss with the days when I don't, and then make the necessary adjustments in my diet.

RECIPES

FROM MY FRIEND
SUSAN HOLT SIMPSON

of Ryland Heights, Kentucky

This yummy recipe comes from my friend Susan Holt Simpson, who is not only a fun friend but an amazing writer. So glad to have met her at a writers' conference— it was one of those divine appointments. I know you'll enjoy her sweet words and sweet brownie recipe. Also, you should check out her blog online: Sweet-Annabelle .blogspot.com.

DID YOU KNOW her when you were a teenager? That long and lean athletic friend who could power up a volleyball serve, eat most of a pizza, and still use a bandanna for a belt? Are you familiar with that blissfully unaware, naturally slender girl who moves with grace through every stage of life—high school, college, workplace, PTA . . . ?

Well, I'm telling you right now, folks, I am not that girl. I have always struggled with my weight, dragging a bag pre-packed with unfavorable genetics on the journey of life. Along the way, I've tried fad diets, expensive weight management programs, and exhausting exercise campaigns. Some of those were wise choices, but some were truly crazy—*cold hot dogs and bananas do not make a great breakfast, even for a teenager.*

As I've grown older, I've become more skilled at seeing myself through the Savior's eyes, enabled by scripture to better cherish being made in His image. But I still often want and wish to look more like the cultural "ideal."

Can you identify?

Not so long ago, I decided to stop worrying about body size. The new-to-me term "thigh gap" might have been the last straw. I tapped out of my lifelong endeavor to maintain a healthy weight and just enjoyed whatever looked delicious. I think you probably know how this turned out. In just a few short months, I gained an additional twenty pounds and outgrew most of my clothes.

It was not pretty, I admit, but I also gained a precious understanding: Jesus loves me at any and every size, but this does not allow me to indulge in an unhealthy and irresponsible lifestyle. I am the Father's well-loved daughter, *and* I'm called to carefully steward the gift of the body He chose for me. This is the balance that brings me true freedom and joy day by day!

Here's a recipe that strikes a balance between the joys of chocolate and . . . zucchini! This is an often-requested treat in my family, and no one minds that the recipe features fresh garden produce.

ZUCCHINI BROWNIES

1 1/2 cups sugar
1/4 cup melted butter
1/4 cup vegetable oil
2 teaspoons vanilla
2 cups flour
1/2 cup cocoa

1 1/2 teaspoons baking
    powder
1 teaspoon salt
2 cups shredded zucchini
1/2 cup chopped walnuts

Preheat oven to 350°F. Grease and cocoa dust a 9 x 9 pan. In a large bowl, combine the sugar, melted butter, oil, and vanilla—set aside.

In another bowl, combine the flour, cocoa, baking powder, and salt. Add the dry ingredients to the sugar mixture in the large bowl and stir to combine. The result will be a crumbly, dry mixture. Now stir in the zucchini shreds and nuts. Keep stirring. A little more . . . The moisture of the zucchini shreds will change the crumbly mixture into a stiff brownie batter. Now you can smooth it into the prepared pan. Bake for about 25 minutes, until it springs back when touched.

If you decide to go all the way, this is the icing recipe:
Melt 1/4 cup of butter and mix in 7 tablespoons of cocoa. To that, add 1 teaspoon of vanilla and 1/4 cup of milk. Stir in 1 cup of powdered sugar. Pour this over warm brownies and allow it to soak in a little bit before cutting and serving.

FROM MY FRIEND
BRENDA ANDERSON
of Dallas, Texas

This avocado chicken salad recipe comes from my Texan buddy Brenda Anderson, who inspires me all the way over here in Indiana. I love following her running feats and healthy tips online. Here's her story and recipe.

HEALTHY EATING IS especially important today due to the extensive exposure we have to so many processed foods in the marketplace, restaurants, and especially fast food. Obesity, diabetes, and many other diseases continue to rise in America. We each need to get the right balance of vitamins, minerals, and other nutrients to provide energy, feel better, and handle everyday stress. Choosing a healthy diet is one of the easiest and best ways to prevent and control many of the common health issues we face today, such as heart disease, high blood pressure, type-2 diabetes, and some types of cancer.

Both of my parents and my brother are diabetic, and I was destined to be diagnosed next at 150 pounds overweight. Two of my cousins passed away from health-related issues that could have been prevented and controlled through a healthier lifestyle. I did not want to be next, and so I took charge of my own life because if I didn't, who would! The changes I made were consistent, primarily healthy eating (the right foods and portion control) along with regular exercise. It saved my life and has changed my life. Healthy eating does not need to be complicated, it simply takes planning, and by preparing the foods yourself, you save money and know exactly what it contains. I continue to learn about the benefits of food and strive to extend my life while I enjoy *life!*

AVOCADO CHICKEN SALAD

1 avocado (peeled/pitted)
1/2 cup plain Greek yogurt
2 tablespoons fresh cilantro (more if desired)
1/2 teaspoon cumin
Salt/pepper (to preferred taste)
1 large lime, juiced
2 cups cooked shredded chicken breasts
2 or 3 green onions, chopped

Combine avocado, Greek yogurt, cilantro, cumin, salt, pepper, and lime juice in food processor. Mix until blended. Add mixture to chicken and green onions and mix well. Refrigerate for 2 hours or overnight. Serve with bread, rolls, pita bread, crackers, or lettuce wraps.

FROM MY FRIEND
ANGELA HERRINGTON
of Marion, Indiana

This yummy smoothie recipe comes from my fabulous friend Angela Herrington, who is also a fellow Hoosier. Angela is committed to helping others get healthy through her online ministry and life coaching. Enjoy her story and recipe!

WHILE EATING HEALTHY is a new thing for me, it has completely shifted my family's energy. We no longer reach for sugary, caffeine-filled drinks to wake us up, or make junk food runs when we are under pressure. Now we reach for fresh fruits and veggies, high-nutrient foods like avocado and almond butter, and lots of water throughout our day. This enormous shift goes well beyond what is in our kitchen. We have also developed a new awareness of how important self-care is for each family member. We eat better. We sleep better. We even spend more time investing in spiritual and emotional wellness.

This protein shake is one of my favorite ways to start the day. It's the perfect balance of natural sweetness and protein that keeps me full for hours.

BANANA SPLIT SHAKE

6 to 9 ounces vanilla unsweetened almond milk
1 to 2 ice cubes
1/2 banana
3 large frozen organic strawberries
1 tablespoon organic almond butter
1/2 serving chocolate protein powder
1/2 serving vanilla protein powder

Fill your personal blender halfway with almond milk. Then add banana, frozen ingredients, almond butter, and top with protein powders. Blend on high 1 to 2 minutes until desired consistency is achieved. Serve immediately or freeze for 15 to 30 minutes and eat with a spoon.

FROM MY FRIEND
LEIGH ANN THOMAS
of Sanford, North Carolina

Submitted by my friend and fellow writer Leigh Ann Thomas, you're sure to enjoy fixing two of her favorite healthy recipes. And for another treat, you might want to check out her blog, Heart Undivided, at leighathomas.com online.

AS A YOUNG MOM with three little girls, my rules were simple: milk and juice instead of soda, and a colorful, balanced dinner plate over junk food. But as the girls entered high school and I became a "sports mom," it was too easy to scoot through a drive-thru window or throw an instant meal into the microwave. Health and nutrition suffered in our busy, overscheduled pace.

Now that two of my girls have started their own families, and my baby is in college, our family is stepping up and encouraging each other to again make wise choices in diet and lifestyle. I am now "soda-free" (great decision for chronic migraines), and have committed to a minimum of thirty minutes of daily exercise. My sweet girls and the gifts of two baby grandsons are serious motivation for healthy living—but the ultimate incentive is to make choices that honor and glorify my Lord!

CHICKEN QUINOA
AND BROCCOLI BAKE

2 cups organic reduced sodium chicken broth

1 cup milk

1/2 cup whole wheat flour

1 cup water

1 cup uncooked quinoa, rinsed

1/2 cup cooked chopped bacon (or to taste)

1 pound boneless skinless chicken breasts

3 teaspoons creole seasoning

3 cups fresh broccoli florets, roughly chopped

1/4 cup shredded Gruyere cheese

Preheat the oven to 400°F and grease a 9 x 13 baking dish. For the sauce, bring the chicken broth and 1/2 cup of milk to a low boil. In a medium bowl, whisk the other 1/2 cup milk, 1 teaspoon of creole seasoning, and the flour; add the mixture to the boiling liquid and whisk until the sauce is smooth and creamy. Add one cup of water, quinoa, and bacon to the sauce and stir to combine. Pour the mixture into the greased baking dish.

Slice the chicken breasts into thin strips and lay the chicken breast strips over the top of the creamy quinoa mixture. Sprinkle with the remaining creole seasoning. Bake uncovered for 30 minutes.

While the casserole is in the oven, cook the broccoli in boiling water for 1 minute until it turns bright green. Drop into cold water to stop the cooking, drain, and set aside.

Remove the casserole from the oven when the quinoa and chicken are cooked and the sauce is thickened. Add the broccoli and stir to combine. Top with the Gruyere and bake for 5 minutes or until cheese is hot and bubbly.

ALL-NATURAL NO-BAKE ENERGY BITES

1/2 cup almond butter
1/3 cup pure honey
1 cup old-fashioned rolled oats
1 cup macadamia nuts, finely chopped
2 teaspoons vanilla
Pinch of sea salt
1 teaspoon instant espresso
1/2 cup organic dark chocolate, finely chopped

In a large bowl, mix all ingredients until well combined; place bowl in fridge for 30 minutes so mixture is easy to handle.

Scoop dough into tablespoon-sized portions and roll into balls. Place balls in an air-tight container and store in fridge or freezer until ready to eat.

FROM MY FRIEND
CAROL BOLEY
of Goodyear, Arizona

I'm so thankful that my buddy Carol Boley was able to share her story and her recipes with us—what a blessing! Amazing that we're such good friends considering her choice in sports teams—the Arizona Wildcats, lol. (Go, Hoosiers!) You can read more from her online at http://carolboley.com/read.html.

MY "FRESHMAN 15" ballooned into the "freshman 50" and hung around for ten years. I loved everything about food . . . the sizzle of a juicy steak, the smell of fresh-baked brownies, and the fun of going out for ice cream with friends. What I didn't love was the jiggle on my belly and thighs and the skyrocketing number on my scales. My life revolved around food. I used it to celebrate victories, soothe heartaches, relieve boredom, silence fears, calm anxiety . . . and my body and spirit paid the price. I was out of control. And I seemed hopeless to help myself.

I enrolled in a fitness class called "Body Dynamics" and soon discovered my body was anything but dynamic. I decided my problem might be always starting a diet on Monday. Perhaps if I started on Tuesday instead? I tried every diet imaginable, including a high-protein regimen. No carbs allowed. One morning I woke up disgusted because I had eaten a fully loaded baked potato. Still in bed, it dawned on me that my offense had actually occurred in my dream. This was getting serious.

My eating was beyond my ability to handle. It was also more than Jenny Craig, NutriSystem, SlimFast, and Dr. Stillman could handle. This called for Jesus. My temptation wasn't solely to overeat. My temptation was to look to something other than Jesus to satisfy me, something other than Jesus in which to delight. He said His grace would be sufficient for me. Did His love and care for me extend to the food I ate and how I handled my emotions? This was my chance to find out. Finally, finally, I surrendered my weakness into His hands and rested in His strength. Sure enough, He came through. Part of the fruit (yum!) of the Spirit is self-control. Exactly what I needed.

In eight months, I lost sixty pounds. They've been gone more than thirty years. How has that been possible? One way is by praying over every morsel that goes in my mouth, including thanking Jesus for taking away guilt, shame, and condemnation. Only He can do that. Another way is learning to enjoy the food God gave us. The following recipes have helped me to do just that. I hope you enjoy them too.

NO-GUILT CHOCOLATE SHAKE

When you want the chocolate, but not the guilt!

3/4 cup unsweetened almond milk, vanilla-flavored
1 tablespoon unsweetened cocoa
1/2 teaspoon vanilla
1 banana (sliced) frozen
15 ice cubes
Stevia to taste

Blend all of the ingredients until smooth. Makes one serving, approximately 100 calories.

DELICIOUS FRUIT SMOOTHIE

1 cup fresh or frozen berries of your choice
1/2 banana (sliced) frozen
1/2 to 1 cup kale
Stevia to taste
1/2 to 1 cup water

Blend all ingredients in blender. If you use fresh berries, add 10 to 12 ice cubes. Blend to desired consistency. Honestly, you won't taste the kale unless you want to! Makes one serving. Approximately 130 calories.

MOUTHWATERING BAKED APPLES

Delicious for dessert, snack, even breakfast!

4 apples (red or green)
1/4 cup chopped pecans
2 tablespoons fresh lemon juice
1 teaspoon ground cinnamon
Stevia to taste

Preheat oven to 350°F. Remove core from each apple, making certain not to cut through the bottom. Combine pecans, lemon juice, Stevia, and cinnamon in small bowl. Spoon mixture into the apples. Place in an 8-inch baking dish. Fill the pan approximately one-fourth of the way up with water. Bake 30 to 40 minutes, depending on size of apples. Serve warm or cold. Makes 4 servings. Approximately 150 calories per serving . . . no charge for the aroma!

FROM MY FRIEND
SALLY HALL
of Fort Worth, Texas

Sometimes you just want some comfort food, so here's a modified version of a favorite comfy food submitted by my sweet and talented friend (and little sister in Christ) Sally Hall. She's a full-time wife, mom, and homeschooler, who is also an anointed writer. To read some of her random musings online, head over to: www.kidsinthehall.wordpress.com.

AS A BUSY STAY-AT-HOME MOM and homeschooler of three kids, finding time to make my health a priority can be a daily battle for me. While I have always loved healthy, fresh foods, I didn't always make the best choices for myself—mostly with sleep and exercise. Yet I had the time to do my best for my kids . . . of course! My big wake-up call came just three months after my mom passed away and I found myself possibly facing the same disease that took her: cancer. Thankfully, my tumor was benign and my thyroid is now working properly.

Now, though, I don't make excuses about my health. I get more sleep, go to bootcamp fitness classes, do Pilates at home with my kids, take bike rides with my eldest son, go on evening walks with my husband, and even play Just Dance with my book club girls! I have found ways to make healthy choices a part of my everyday routine. I'm not perfect, but I most definitely feel better. Plus, I'm (hopefully) setting my kids up for better lifestyle choices with my example of taking care of both myself and them.

This recipe is a great example of that. It's a lighter version of my favorite comfort food—creamy potato soup. By substituting half of the potatoes for cauliflower and using almond milk, I get the creamy goodness without the guilt. Plus, my family eats it without realizing what they're missing!

CREAMY POTATO-FLOWER SOUP

1 large head cauliflower, chopped
1 pound red potatoes, peeled and cubed
1 onion, finely chopped
3 cloves garlic, finely chopped
32 ounces chicken broth
2 cups unsweetened, unflavored almond milk
8 ounces shredded mozzarella cheese
4 ounces chopped turkey bacon or turkey bacon bits
Salt and pepper (to taste)

Put cauliflower, potatoes, onion, and garlic into a slow cooker. Pour broth over the mixture. Cover and cook on high for 3 or 4 hours. Mash mixture and add almond milk, then stir. Cover and cook for an additional 20 minutes. Serve and top each bowl with cheese and turkey bacon bits.

FROM MY FRIEND
LAURIE EPPS
of Anderson, South Carolina

My friend and colleague Laurie Epps (we refer to each other as one another's cheerleader) has blessed us with her story and a yummy soup recipe that I recently made and loved. You're in for a treat. To read more about her fitness journey, follow her at http://1writerlaurieepps .blogspot.com/online.

I WASN'T ALWAYS HEAVY. In fact, in my late teens I had anorexia and was a bit of an athlete. At that time, my exercise of choice was running, and I even competed in marathons. I thought I was so fat at 108 pounds. I worked out five to six days a week at that time, and lived on salads and Diet Sprite. I couldn't eat too little, exercise too much, or weigh myself too often. I used to weigh myself like I was gold and silver, counting every ounce. At a whopping 108 pounds with my 5'11" frame, I was a skeleton at best. Yet I looked in the mirror and saw a lie. Over the years, I fought that same battle over and over again.

Working out carried into my adulthood, except while I was bearing children. With my two oldest daughters, I managed to lose most of my baby weight by the time they were two years old. However, there was always that that battle with those last, pesky ten to thirty pounds until I moved to South

Carolina from California a decade later. A little bit of weight was starting to creep up on me from a massive fibroid in my uterus that I was unaware of until it manifested into some of the worst female trouble I'd had in my life. Six surgeries, three miscarriages, and the birth of my youngest child had me on medically ordered bed rest for close to five years. At the end of that, I learned of my uterine cancer and had my hysterectomy that summer on break from college. All that time in bed led to massive gains on the scale, and by the end of that journey, I'd gained another 90 pounds, for a total weight gain of close to 140 pounds.

Against the odds, I graduated from college two years later. I decided that as a newly single mom, I needed to regain control of my weight and my health. I've been going to the gym regularly, and I've lost my first 17 pounds. For the first time in a long while, I'm hopeful. I can lose the next 120 pounds, and I'll continue to astound myself and others with my transformation. God is so good. He wouldn't have carried me so far to leave me in the state I was in. I started a blog, too, to track my progress, and to put myself out in the community. Together we can do this.

MAMA'S TEXAS BLACK BEAN SOUP

1 chicken broth carton (32 ounces)
2 cans diced tomatoes (14.5 ounces)*
2 cans corn, rinsed (or small bag frozen corn)
2 cans black beans (14.5 ounces), rinsed and drained
1 teaspoon cumin
2 teaspoon chili powder
2 cloves fresh garlic
3–4 bay leaves

Pour chicken broth and diced tomatoes in slow cooker. Rinse and drain corn, black beans, and add into slow cooker. Add cumin, chili powder, and garlic to soup. Either place bay leaves on top, or crush them and mix them into soup. Place slow cooker on its low setting, and let it simmer at least 6 to 8 hours. Serve in bowls when you get home. We like it with corn bread, though it's not as healthy then.

Serves 12 at 243 calories per serving.

We love to eat this recipe on autumn and winter evenings. Since they're the busiest nights of the year, having a recipe this easy is a real plus.

*Note: A variation is to get 2 cans of diced tomatoes (14.5 ounces), 1 small can of mild green chilies (4 ounces), and chives from the produce department (chopped).

FROM MY FRIEND MARGARET MCSWEENEY
of Barrington Hills, Illinois

Oh, we are so blessed to have my talented friend and culinary cutie, Margaret McSweeney, share with us her story and one of her favorite healthy recipes. She is the host of a show in which chefs, cookbook authors, and foodies share their recipes and cooking tips, as well as answer questions from those of us who are "cooking challenged." Go here http://kitchenchat.info/ to learn more. I am thankful for so many friends who are so gifted and gracious.

THIS IS A DISH FROM MY HEART to your home. It's easy to make too! I am a three-year breast cancer survivor, and healthy eating has become an important part of my culinary journey. I host "Kitchen Chat" as a way to honor my late father, who was an incredible gourmet home chef. My biggest regret in life was not going into the kitchen with my father to learn how to cook. He passed away twenty-five years ago in mid-life, and I am now discovering what his joy of cooking was all about. Please visit me at my website, Kitchenchat.info, and always remember to take a moment and savor the day!

ZUCCHINI CAPPELLINI D'ANGELO MARINARA

This "pasta" dish makes nutritious taste delicious!

1 1/2 zucchinies per serving

1 tablespoon olive oil

2–3 garlic cloves

2 diced tomatoes per serving (or low-sodium canned tomatoes)

1 tablespoon white wine

1 tablespoon red wine

Salt (I recommend using Himalayan salt.)

Pepper

Instead of pasta, you can actually make zucchini pasta with a spiral slicer. Use 1 1/2 small zucchinies per serving. Sauté the spiraled zucchini in olive oil and fresh garlic and set aside.

For the marinara sauce, which I like to call "Savor the Day" sauce, use two diced tomatoes of your choice per serving. In a sauté pan, sweat several cloves of garlic in olive oil. Add tomatoes and simmer until tomatoes turn pink and tender. Add a few splashes of red and white wine. Salt and pepper to taste. Simmer a few more minutes and pour over a bed of zucchini pasta.

(Thank you to Lynn Gentile, who helped me create this recipe).

FROM MY FRIEND PAIGE SNEDEKER

of Thonotosassa, Florida

I met my buddy Paige Snedeker, a talented artist and writer, at the Florida Christian Writers Conference in 2013, and we became fast friends. Her love of life and sweet spirit makes me want to be a better person. Paige has had her share of health obstacles in her life, as she suffers from a rare neuromuscular disease that has progressively claimed the use of her arms and legs and her ability to breathe without a tracheotomy, but she believes that eating healthy is one key to helping her feel stronger. I'm so glad she was willing to share a bit of her reasons for choosing to eat healthy and two of her family's favorite recipes.

SINCE I STARTED EATING HEALTHIER, my body has improved in many ways. My digestive system has been working much better. Also, I have skin problems. My face kept breaking out really bad. So I changed my diet and started eating a lot more greens, which helped clear up my face. My body feels stronger since I have made these changes in my diet.

ANN-MARIE'S YUMMY SALAD
WITH MISO DRESSING

2 heads romaine lettuce

2 to 3 stalks celery

1/2 cucumber (You can leave the skin on it if it's organic.)

3 large tomatoes, diced

1/2 red onion, diced

2/3 7-ounce block of Greek feta cheese, softened

2/3 cup sweetened cranberries

1/2 cup raw pumpkin seeds

Miso Dressing

2 tablespoons non-gmo miso (Cold Mountain Light
Yellow)

6 tablespoons extra-virgin olive oil (cold-pressed)

2 tablespoons lemon juice

1 tablespoon maple syrup (optional)

Tear romaine lettuce into small pieces and add finely chopped celery and cucumber. Add diced tomatoes and red onion. Next, add crumbled feta cheese, cranberries, pumpkin seeds, and miso dressing. Toss and let sit for a few minutes. Serves 4 to 8 people.

CHIA PUDDING

1/2 cup chia black seeds

1 cup cashew, almond, or coconut milk

1 teaspoon vanilla

1/4 teaspoon cinnamon

1 tablespoon grade-B maple syrup

Pour all ingredients into a quart jar, shake for 30 seconds, and refrigerate overnight. In the morning, mix with a little more milk. It can be heated. Add walnuts or almonds, raisins, blueberries, or whatever fruit you like. (Chia seeds are high in Omega 3s and fiber—great for digestion.)

FROM MY FRIEND
LA-TAN MURPHY
Raleigh, North Carolina

I am so thankful my adorable friend La-Tan Roland Murphy, who is not only a great cook but also an amazing author and teacher of God's Word, agreed to share her story and recipes with us. I know you'll enjoy them!

RECENTLY, I'VE REALIZED it took years to shift into my larger-sized love machine, and I need to give my slower metabolism time to shift back—slowly, in order to keep the weight off. For me, making small changes in my diet has proven most powerful. I now think about what foods will give me the most energy, and the best clarity of mind, before worrying about weight loss. I want to *feel* my best, so I can *be* my *best*.

Weight loss has happened faster because I'm most concerned these days about fueling my body with great-tasting, healthy foods—like my Quinoa Salad! Yum! And there are just as many laughs shared with good friends over this power-packed, protein-enriched dinner by candlelight, as there are with any other fat-ladened dish. Fun happens, and I feel my best!

QUINOA SALAD

1 cup quinoa, boiled and drained

1 teaspoon sea salt

Dash black pepper (to taste)

16 ounces feta cheese, crumbled

1 fresh lime, squeeze juice out

1 fresh lemon, squeeze juice out

1 small bunch of fresh basil, chopped

1 bunch green onion, chopped finely

1 can black beans, rinse and drain

3 tablespoons extra-virgin olive oil

2 cups baby spinach leaves, rinse, drain, chop

1 bell pepper, chopped

1 small can of shoe peg corn, drain

2 tablespoons of freshly crushed garlic

1 small container of cherry tomatoes, rinse and cut into
halves

Toss all of the above ingredients together. Serve at room temperature or serve after chilling.

I often add grilled chicken on top (see following chicken recipe).

GRILLED ITALIAN MARINATED CHICKEN

12 chicken tenders
1 small bottle soy sauce
1 small bottle zesty Italian dressing

Pour dressing and soy-sauce over chicken and marinate overnight. Grill or oven-bake at 400°F until tender. Chop or serve chicken tenders on top of quinoa salad. Sprinkle top with your favorite grated cheese (I like to use sharp cheddar). *Yummy!* Serves 6 adults healthy portions!

APPENDIX

SCRIPTURES TO STAND ON WHILE ON THIS JOURNEY

(in reference to the Write Your Vision devotional entry)

When you're feeling discouraged, not sure if you can continue on the wellness journey . . .

- "You are of God, little children, and have overcome them, because He who is in you is greater than he who is in the world" (1 John 4:4 NKJV).
- "'What do you mean, "If I can"?' Jesus asked. 'Anything is possible if a person believes'" (Mark 9:23 NLT).
- "Christ gives me the strength to face anything" (Philippians 4:13 CEV).
- "'Haven't I commanded you? Strength! Courage! Don't be timid; don't get discouraged. GOD, your God, is with you every step you take'" (Joshua 1:9 MSG).
- "But those who trust in the LORD will find new strength. They will soar high on wings like eagles. They will run and not grow weary. They will walk and not faint" (Isaiah 40:31 NLT).

When you need encouragement and strength to consistently work out . . .

- "I don't know about you, but I'm running hard for the finish line. I'm giving it everything I've got. No sloppy living for me! I'm staying alert and in top condition" (1 Corinthians 9:26 MSG).

- "Therefore, since we are surrounded by such a huge crowd of witnesses to the life of faith, let us strip off every weight that slows us down, especially the sin that so easily trips us up. And let us run with endurance the race God has set before us" (Hebrews 12:1 NLT).

- "Workouts in the gymnasium are useful, but a disciplined life in God is far more so, making you fit both today and forever. You can count on this. Take it to heart. This is why we've thrown ourselves into this venture so totally" (1 Timothy 4:8–9 MSG).

When you're having trouble resisting the urge to overeat . . .

- "No temptation has seized you except what is common to man. And God is faithful; he will not let you be tempted beyond what you can bear. But when you are tempted, he will also provide a way out so that you can stand up under it" (1 Corinthians 10:13 NIV).

- "For God has not given us a spirit of fear and timidity, but of power, love, and self-discipline" (2 Timothy 1:7 NLT).

SLEEP WELL

Dr. James B. Maas, author of *Power Sleep* (HarperCollins, 1999) suggests the following fifteen sleep strategies in case you have trouble falling asleep at night:

1. Reduce stress as much as possible.
2. Exercise regularly—but not within three hours of going to bed.
3. Eat a healthy diet.
4. Keep mentally stimulated during the day.
5. Clear your mind at bedtime.
6. Try some bedtime relaxation techniques.
7. Stop smoking.
8. Reduce caffeine intake—especially close to bedtime.
9. Take a warm bath before bedtime.
10. Avoid alcohol near bedtime.
11. Learn to value sleep.
12. Maintain a relaxing atmosphere in the bedroom.
13. Establish a bedtime ritual.
14. Avoid trying too hard to get sleep.
15. If necessary, consult a sleep specialist.

CHOOSE YOUR GYM WISELY

First off, if the gym isn't close to your home or your workplace, you probably won't go as regularly, so make sure the gym you join is convenient. Also, it's good to visit it at the time you'll most likely be working out each day. How busy is it? Will you have access to the machines you need? Is there a line to use the treadmills?

Make sure you take a tour of the gym before joining, and while touring, keep your senses on high alert.

Using Your Eyes
- Look for a clean environment, a friendly staff, and well-maintained equipment.
- Check the benches and machines for fraying cables and stitching. Look at the cardio machines for wear and tear.
- It's also a good idea to scan the walls for instructors' certifications through the American College of Sports Medicine (ACSM), IDEA Health & Fitness Association, American Council on Exercise (ACE), or Aerobics and Fitness Association of America (AFAA).
- If you don't see any certifications posted, ask about the personal trainers'/fitness specialists' experience and education.

Using Your Ears

- Do you hear a lot of laughter and visiting going on inside the gym? That's a good thing. Who wants to go to a gym that is less than friendly?

- Listen to the equipment that is in use—is it making strange noises, like it needs an overhaul? If it is, the equipment is probably in bad shape and in need of repair. Beware! (If the gym owners aren't willing to take care of their equipment, they probably won't be too attentive to you, either.)

- While your ears are perked up, ask others who are working out if they are satisfied with the health club. Ask for specific examples as to why they like or dislike the gym. You can learn much from a "regular."

Using Your Nose

- Does the health club smell "yucky"? If it smells like dirty sweat socks, you might want to keep looking at other health clubs. Remember, you want the health club you choose to be inviting and pleasant. If it stinks, you'll be less motivated to visit regularly.

- On the other hand, do you smell a citrus aroma coming from the outskirts of the gym? Follow your nose. It might just lead you to a groovy juice bar, which is a great place to relax and socialize after a hard workout.

Using Your Hands

- Run your fingers over the various weight benches . . . Is the leather cracked? Ripping? Sweaty from the last person who used it? (Eww.) Again, if the club owners aren't maintaining their equipment, the club may be in financial trouble or under poor management.
- A gym and its team of fitness professionals can be a real turbo boost on your path toward a healthy, fit body, but you must choose wisely.
- Lastly and most importantly, know that God wants to be involved in every part of your life—even which gym you choose—so involve Him. Ask for God's help in your search for the best gym.

Beware of language from gym personnel like, "This offer is only good today." That's unwarranted sales pressure, and it's probably not even true. If you are not ready to commit to joining that day, chances are you will be able to get that "today only" special another day. Also, be leery of gimmicky promotions that may let you join for a small fee but then charge you extra for classes and the use of the gym's pools, saunas, etc. So be sure to ask what the membership fee includes.

It's also wise to compare the membership prices of other gyms in your area. Is the gym you're considering offering a comparable membership fee? If it's too high, move on to another gym. (I also always use Yelp to read reviews from other gym patrons.)

ABOUT THE AUTHOR

MICHELLE MEDLOCK ADAMS is an award-winning journalist and author, earning top honors from the Associated Press, the Society of Professional Journalists and the Hoosier State Press Association. Author of over 70 books and a popular blogger for Guideposts, Michelle also helps others write their message, serving as a ghostwriter for some of today's most effective ministers, celebrities, and fitness experts. And, Michelle served as the health and fitness columnist for *Christian Single* magazine for several years; wrote articles for Fitserv.com; and developed many health/fitness stories for magazines such as *Energy, Christian Health, HomeLife, The Dollar Stretcher, American Cheerleader* and CBN.com online.

As a former AFAA certified fitness trainer and aerobics instructor, Michelle taught fitness at the Bloomington, IN., YMCA, the Indiana University Fit program, Downtown Fit in Bloomington, and Fit For Life in Bedford, IN. Today, Michelle is a certified Group Fitness and Bootcamp Instructor through American Sports & Fitness Association and enjoys teaching various fitness classes at Priority Fitness in Bedford, IN.

Michelle is also a much sought after teacher at writers' conferences around the nation and has served as an adjunct professor at Taylor University twice over the past few years. She also loves speaking to women's groups, youth groups, and congregations, encouraging others to follow God and discover their destinies in Him. She is married to her high school sweetheart, Jeff, and they have two daughters, Abby and Allyson, as well as one miniature dachshund and four cats.

To learn more, go to www.michellemedlockadams.com online.

IF YOU ENJOYED THIS BOOK, WILL YOU CONSIDER SHARING THE MESSAGE WITH OTHERS?

Mention the book in a blog post or through Facebook, Twitter, Pinterest, or upload a picture through Instagram.

Recommend this book to those in your small group, book club, workplace, and classes.

Head over to facebook.com/worthypublishing, "LIKE" the page, and post a comment as to what you enjoyed the most.

Tweet "I recommend reading #LoveAndCareForTheOneAndOnlyYou by @Inwritergirl // @worthypub"

Pick up a copy for someone you know who would be challenged and encouraged by this message.

Write a book review online.

WORTHY®

PUBLISHING

Visit us at worthypublishing.com

twitter.com/worthypub

worthypub.tumblr.com

facebook.com/worthypublishing

pinterest.com/worthypub

instagram.com/worthypub

youtube.com/worthypublishing